I f...
helpful!
- Gabriel

Brilliant Faith

How Smart It Is To Believe in Jesus

S. Gabriel Tew

RIVER BIRCH PRESS

Daphne, Alabama

ISBN 978-1-956365-25-2 (print)
ISBN 978-1-956365-26-9 (e-book)

For Worldwide Distribution
Printed in the U.S.A.

River Birch Press
P.O. Box 868, Daphne, AL 36526

Dedicated to the Tew Crew

(Sharlene, Sidney, Nathan, Kristin, Jacob, Luke, & Janna).

God has used you immensely to help me grow

and exercise my faith.

Contents

Prologue

Two or Three Witnesses

By the mouths of two or three witnesses the matter shall be established (Deut. 19:15).

But when the Helper comes, whom I shall send to you from the Father, the Spirit of truth who proceeds from the Father, He will testify of Me. And you also will bear witness because you have been with Me from the beginning (John 15:26-27).

The Holy Spirit also witnesses to us (Heb. 10:15).

And we [the apostles] are His [Jesus'] witnesses to these things, and so also is the Holy Spirit whom God has given to those who obey Him (Acts 5:32).

In a land of foolish judges, the day arrived for them to hear the case. So did Joshua. And so did Kosmonio. Joshua and Kosmonio sat at tables on opposite sides at the front of the courtroom, facing the judge, who sat before them behind a lofty desk.

The judge called the court to order and opened proceedings. "I will now hear the case of Joshua versus Kosmonio. The accuser may present his case."

Kosmonio rose and presented his case against Joshua, claiming that Joshua failed to deliver merchandise for which Kosmonio paid. He made the same presentation he had made weeks before in regional court. His presentation was just as impressive as before. He concluded by saying, "That is my case, honorable judge." Kosmonio sat, beaming with snide confidence.

Then the judge did something judges of that land never did, taking everyone by surprise, especially Kosmonio. The judge fastened his eyes upon Joshua and said, "Now the accused may present his defense."

Joshua eagerly rose. "Thank you, your honor. I was not allowed to speak in our regional trial. That is the reason the judge ruled in Kosmonio's favor and the reason I have appealed my case to you. I will prove to you, sir, that not only did the accuser receive the goods he claims he did not, but he did not pay for them, though he claims that he did."

Joshua approached the judge and handed him a document. "This is the receipt for the merchandise Kosmonio received. At the bottom are two lines. One has Kosmonio's signature acknowledging receipt of the goods, and the other line is where I would sign for receiving payment. As you can see, the customer, the accuser, received the goods but I, the accused, did not receive payment."

The judge lifted his eyes from the document and fixed them on the accuser. "Kosmonio, can you offer any proof that you paid for the goods received?"

"No, I cannot," Kosmonio said, embarrassed that he could not support his claim.

The judge called for a recess, left the room, and returned shortly with his decision. "Given the evidence presented, I find for the defendant. Kosmonio, you have exactly four weeks to pay Joshua for the goods received. If you do not pay, you will be confined to debtors' prison that very day."

Kosmonio was disappointed, Joshua ecstatic. Justice had been served, and the judge became known as the Brilliant Judge for one simple reason: he listened to both sides of a case before making his decision. It seems elementary, but in a land of foolish judges, that's all it took to be known as brilliant.

Two or three witnesses—the Holy Spirit,

the Bible, and someone like me.

This book will help you hear those three witnesses.

As you read, your faith will become brilliant

in a land of foolish judgments.

Section 1

The Five Facets of Brilliant Faith

What gives a diamond its brilliance is the light that radiates from it. Jewelers make cuts in gems called facets so the light can have added windows through which to shine.

The first section of this book, which includes the first five chapters, is about the five facets of brilliant faith. Each facet is a window through which the brilliant light of faith in Christ shines. Each facet matches one of the five letters in the word faith. Together, they shine forth a more complete understanding of Christian faith than I've ever seen elsewhere. My prayer is that *Brilliant Faith* will shine God's light clearly for you as you read it. Here are the five facets and their defining statements:

Familiar: Being familiar with God is the basis of brilliant faith.

Aware: Brilliant faith is relevant because it makes us aware of God in our current situations.

Invoke: To invoke God is the expression of brilliant faith.

Trust: To trust God is the essence of brilliant faith.

Heed: To heed God is to walk out brilliant faith.

—1—

Familiar

*Being familiar with God is
the basis of brilliant faith.*

Faith without Basis Is Dead

Faith is always based on something. It can be based on a mathematical probability, a feeling, a fact, or a majority opinion. We can base our faith on a desire, a timeless truth, or a lie we believe to be true. Even if we aren't conscious of what it is, we always have a reason, a basis, for what we believe and trust. Faith always has a basis. The question is: Is that basis dependable?

The basis of brilliant faith is our knowledge of God, our being familiar with Him. God is completely reliable, so if our familiarity with Him is accurate, then the basis of our faith is completely reliable. God will always be stronger than the faith we have in Him. Everything doesn't depend upon our faith. Still, faith does have excellent value, and the basis of our faith is our familiarity with God. Faith will never be stronger than its basis. It's only as strong as its basis. Without accurate knowledge of the living God, faith is dead.

> **God is completely reliable, so if our familiarity with Him is accurate, then the basis of our faith is completely reliable.**

Getting Familiar with God

How much we know about God is important, but even more significant is what we know about Him. We don't have to know everything about God. We can't. He's far too vast and complex for us to understand. Since we can't know everything about Him, we just need to know the right things about Him. I struggled in deciding which of God's attributes to include in this chapter. I chose to list the ones most meaningful to me. These are my favorites, but they are all available to everyone. The list could include dozens of things I love about God, but I've whittled it down to seven:

1. God really does love me immensely.

He doesn't need to work at loving as a husband and wife must work to keep the flames of their love burning for each other. God is love. He loves just by being Himself. Love flows from Him, just as a light shines light from itself.

He loved me while I was rebelling against Him and trying to exclude Him from my life. I spent my early years as a boy and as a young man working to satisfy my own lustful and prideful pleasures, even though I knew it displeased the Lord of all creation, my Creator. Meanwhile, He wanted me, protected me, pursued me, and rescued me from the darkness of my destructive choices, establishing me in His light and love. God did all that because in His heart was a yearning love for me.

For a moment, however, Jesus—God who became a man—didn't want to suffer the torture He knew awaited Him in His sacrifice to pay my ransom. Still, He yielded His will to the will of the heavenly Father and chose to express His love to me by giving His life for me. Thus, God has expressed His love for me and all of us both naturally and by sacrificial choice.

God demonstrates His own love toward us, in that while we were still sinners, Christ died for us. Much more then, having now been justified by His blood, we shall be saved from wrath through Him. For if when we were enemies we were reconciled to God through the death of His Son, much more, having been reconciled, we shall be saved by His life (Rom. 5:8-10).

Can a mother forget her nursing child? Can she feel no love for the child she has borne? But even if that were possible, I would not forget you! See, I have written your name on the palms of my hands (Isa. 49:15-16 NLT).

2. He has forgiven me for every wrong I've ever done.

God hasn't removed just my feeling of guilt, but my guilt itself. I often notice people seeking relief from feeling guilty, as if the only problem is an emotional one. While we often do carry false guilt (blame and shame for something not our fault), my problem was not merely feeling guilty. It was being guilty. Even so, God completely solved my guilt problem. He did it by forgiving me for every sin I've ever committed. It's as if He's said, "You have wronged Me, other people, and even yourself. But I forgive all of that because My Son paid the penalty for all of it by His death on the cross. And you have believed in Him, accepted Him, and received His salvation." God didn't just soothe the pain of my guilty feelings. He removed my guilt by removing my sin. He has dealt with the very root cause of my guilty feelings.

As far as the east is from the west, so far has He removed our transgressions from us (Ps. 103:12).

"Come now, and let us reason together," says the Lord, "Though your sins are like scarlet, they shall be as white as snow; though they are red like crimson, they shall be as wool" (Isa. 1:18).

All have sinned and fall short of the glory of God (Rom. 3:23).

The wages of sin is death, but the gift of God is eternal life (Rom. 6:23).

In Him we have redemption through His blood, the forgiveness of sins, according to the riches of His grace (Eph. 1:7).

3. He constantly shows grace and mercy to me.

It just isn't fair the way God treats me. I deserve to live in shame for the way I've lived. Because of my lifestyle in my younger years, it's only fair that I would have several children with several different mothers to whom I would pay child support and would have the challenge of helping support several different households. However, I'm married to a lovely, godly lady, and she and I have six children.

I could have several DUIs (driving under the influence of alcohol or other drugs) on my driving record and all the added consequences—legal, financial, social, and professional—that go along with such behavior, but my driving record is clean in that regard. It would only be fair if my life were different in the worst ways from the way it is. God hasn't been fair to me. Instead, He's given me His undeserved favor and protection, treating me mercifully every day in every way.

While we can't expect God to remove all the consequences of our negative actions, and I have endured some of those consequences, my personal story is written on pages of mercy with the ink of grace The shower of blessings I've experienced and still enjoy in this life is just the tip of the iceberg. What awaits me in eternity is a forever-long experience with no consequences for my sins but complete joy, peace, and love in the presence of Almighty God, who forgave me and freed me from what I deserve.

The Lord is merciful and gracious, slow to anger, and abounding in mercy (Ps. 103:8).

For as the heavens are high above the earth, so great is His mercy toward those who fear Him (Ps. 103:11).

4. He will never leave me.

God is closer to me than anyone else is. My wife and I are remarkably close, but God lives in me. He's at the very place where I think and feel. I don't have to make a sound when I call out to God. I can reach Him with a thought, and I have His promise that He will always be that close to me.

I will never leave you nor forsake you (Heb. 13:5).

For the Lord your God will personally go ahead of you. He will neither fail you nor abandon you (Deut. 31:6 NLT).

Where can I go from your Spirit? Where can I flee from your presence? If I go up to the heavens, you are there; if I make my bed in the depths, you are there. If I rise on the wings of the dawn, if I settle on the far side of the sea, even there your hand will guide me, your right hand will hold me fast (Ps. 139:7-10).

5. He is my provider.

God is aware of every need I have, even the ones I'm not aware of myself. He is aware of and cares about every need I have. Furthermore, He is unlimited in His ability to meet my needs. His provision is always in abundance, never lacking, not even just a little bit.

The Lord is my shepherd, I shall not be in want (Ps. 23:1 NIV).

My God shall supply all your need according to His riches in glory by Christ Jesus (Phil. 4:19).

He who did not spare His own Son, but delivered Him up for

us all, how shall He not with Him also freely give us all things?
(Rom. 8:32-33)

Blessed be the God and Father of our Lord Jesus Christ, who has blessed us with every spiritual blessing in the heavenly places in Christ (Eph. 1:3).

6. He is holy.

Holy means "set apart." If something is holy, it has been set apart for God's purpose. God is holy because there is none like Him; He is set apart from all others. Nothing can compare to Him. He is unique in all the highest and best ways. He is *the* Creator, *the* Savior, *the* Judge, *the* Everlasting God. He stands alone in every way. None can stand against Him as His enemy or beside Him as His peer. He calls me to be holy—to be set apart for His purposes—and gives me His Holy Spirit to dwell in me and lead me in a holy lifestyle of thoughts, words, and actions.

The Lord sits in majesty in Jerusalem, exalted above all the nations. Let them praise your great and awesome name. Your name is holy! (Ps. 99:2-3 NLT)

7. He is my master trainer and leader.

God knows me better than anyone does. He put me together and breathed His breath of life into me. He has plans for me and knows best how to mold me and prepare me for them. He orders my steps, corrects my course, and leads me in the way I should go. His timing is perfect, and He knows how to stretch me or comfort me when needed.

You formed my inward parts; You covered me in my mother's womb (Ps. 139:13).

He restores my soul; He leads me in paths of righteous for His name's sake (Ps. 23:3).

The Bullseye

The real bullseye of *Familiar* is God Himself. The attributes I've listed are important, and so are many others that I didn't. However, all those things are like the rings around the bullseye. To be familiar with God, we need to pursue an intimate relationship with Him.

Studying His Word is vital because there we see the way He deals with people, the way He thinks, the way He speaks, and what He says to us. Also vital is being in close fellowship with Him. I love my time alone with the Lord in the mornings when I talk with Him and seek Him for answers. I also enjoy time with other believers, worshiping, praying, or studying the Bible together. Taking evening walks, especially on the beach, just to talk with the Lord, is also enjoyable. Everyone connects with God in unique ways, but the point is to pursue Him and get to know Him.

It's easy to get focused on some of the rings on the target—good things like worship music, gifted Bible teachers, even learning Scripture—but the bullseye is God Himself. He, and nothing else, is the central focus for the basis of brilliant faith.

Personal Application

- List your seven favorite characteristics of God and find Scriptures to validate each one.

- Try to expand your familiarity with God by learning something new about Him. You can do this through searching

the Scriptures and meditating on and praying about something you haven't noticed before.

~2~

Aware

Brilliant faith is relevant because it makes us aware of God in our current situations.

It's the Lord!

Jesus had been crucified, had risen from the grave, and had shown Himself to His disciples multiple times. Peter and some of the other disciples are out fishing not far off the shore of the Sea of Galilee when they hear a man shouting out to them. "Fellows, have you caught any fish?" They shout back that they have not.

Jesus says, "Cast the net on the right side of the boat, and you will find some" (John 21:6).

They do, and the net fills up with fish so that they can't even get it into the boat. "It's the Lord!" John shouts. Too excited to wait for the boat to take him to shore, Peter jumps in and swims to Jesus (John 21:7).

Some of those same guys were out fishing some three years earlier. They had been fishing all night and caught nothing. They were cleaning their boats when Jesus stepped on to Peter's to teach the multitude of people who had gathered at water's edge to hear His teachings. When He finished addressing the crowd, He told Peter to go out and cast his nets again. They had just spent an unsuccessful night in those waters, but out of respect to this rabbi, Peter went out a ways and cast his net. Soon the net was so filled with fish that it was tearing, and the boat was sinking.

Peter was astonished and not being familiar with Jesus, was afraid and begged Him to depart from him, "for I am a sinful man," he said.

"Don't be afraid," Jesus assured him. "From now on you will catch men."

That was the call Jesus extended to Peter, James, and John. They accepted and began a three-year journey of becoming increasingly familiar with Jesus. (See Luke 5:1-11.)

Three years later, Peter recognized that it was Jesus standing on the shore calling out to His disciples. He connected the dots. He was familiar with Jesus now, so he recognized Him. Because Peter was aware of Jesus' presence, he rushed to be with Him.

———————

To *recognize* means "to readmit something familiar into our cognition" (re: again; cognize: know).

What we've known in a previous setting is now part of our thinking in this setting. It is precisely what happens when we are familiar with God, and we therefore sense His presence and involvement in our situation: we include Him in our thought processes.

Ongoing recognition is awareness. To be aware of God is to continually recognize Him. When we're aware of God, His presence and involvement influence our every thought.

> **When we're aware of God, His presence and involvement influence our every thought.**

11

Open My Eyes That I May See

The king of Syria learned that it was Elisha, the Hebrew prophet, who had been tipping off the king of Israel each time the Syrians made plans to attack. One night the Syrian king sent horses and chariots and a huge army, and they surrounded the town where Elisha lived. When Elisha's servant rose early that next morning and went outside, fear struck him at the sight of the army; he asked his master what they should do (2 Kings 6:8-14).

> *"Do not fear, for those who are with us are more than those who are with them," Elisha told him. And Elisha prayed, and said, 'Lord, I pray, open his eyes that he may see.' Then the Lord opened the eyes of the young man, and he saw. And behold, the mountain was full of horses and chariots of fire all around Elisha. When the Syrians came down to him, Elisha prayed to the Lord, saying, 'Strike this people, I pray, with blindness.' And He struck them with blindness according to the word of Elisha"* (2 Kings 6:16-18).

As a prophet with a special gift from God, Elisha was able to see God's presence and involvement in his situation. We may not always see with the same clarity as Elisha did when he saw the heavenly army that day, but as Spirit-filled believers of Jesus Christ, we can have an awareness that God is present and involved in our situations. Awareness of God opens a portal into the amazing world of what He is doing in our lives. We just must remember to be alert and ready to recognize Him. When we are, God will open our spiritual eyes to recognize that He is present and at work. Any time we feel we are more aware of our enemy than we are of God, let's pray, "Lord, please open my eyes that I may see."

Fruit of Awareness

When we're aware of God, we can open our hearts to Him and allow Him to work in us. Here are some of the fruits of surrendering to Him in this way.

Encouragement

After giving the instructions for Joshua and the Israelites to familiarize themselves with God's laws, the Lord gave Joshua these instructions: "Be strong and courageous. Do not be terrified or dismayed . . . for the Lord your God is with you wherever you go" (Josh.1:9 AMP). After becoming thoroughly familiar with God's law, they were to take something else into the battles they would fight—strength and courage.

The Hebrew word translated *be courageous* means "to be alert." What did the Lord want them to be alert about? I believe He wanted them to be alert to His presence. What would've given them more courage than knowing that God was with them and working on their behalf? That's why He followed up the command with the encouraging truth that He would be with them wherever they went.

The best kind of courage comes from knowing that God is with us and for us and against our enemy. It was critical that the Israelites be aware of God's presence and involvement in their situations, and it's critical for us to remember the same in ours. Jesus has promised us, His disciples, that He will always be with us (Matt. 28:20). God infuses us with courage by making us aware that He is with us.

Conviction and Correction

The Latin word for "convict" is a combination of *con*, which means "with" and *vicere*, which means "wrong," or "to be with wrong." The Holy Spirit convicts us, showing us where we are wrong and how to respond to that wrong. One of the great advantages of belonging to Christ is that our conviction leads to correction rather than condemnation (1 Cor. 8:1). As a result, when we are convicted (found to be with wrong) in our hearts, we soon find our hearts in the correct condition as we cooperate with the Holy Spirit's corrective leading.

Being aware of God's presence means we are more sensitive to the convicting and correcting whispers of the Holy Spirit. What a benefit to have God's Spirit dwelling in us as believers in Jesus! Being aware of God's presence and involvement is how we take advantage of that priceless benefit.

Comfort

My dad passed away one Saturday, my mom the following Tuesday. Losing both of my parents within three days of each other was painful enough. To make matters worse, I had regrets concerning my dad. My relationship with him had been rocky at times. He and I had made our peace with one another, but I was still dealing with remorse as I grieved his death. I knew he was with the Lord now because his faith was in Jesus, and I knew I would see him again because my faith is in Jesus. I also knew that since our reunion would be in the age when there would be no more tears, any trace of pain we had caused each other would be gone forever. Still, I battled regret.

During the two-and-a-half-year period following their deaths, I became more consistently aware of God's presence than ever before. I spent hundreds of early morning hours alone with God. In those quiet hours before dawn, He comforted me by revealing some truths to me:

- If my dad were alive on earth, he would completely forgive me for every wrong I had made toward him. I knew this was true because whatever shortcomings my dad had, one of his strengths was that he always was quick to forgive.

- My dad was in a place now where his consciousness had transcended earthly thinking. Wrongs done to him no longer had a place in his mind.

- I had hurt my dad while he was here. He was a child of God, and he was my father. My actions at times were wrong, which may not seem a comforting thought. It wasn't, by itself, but the Holy Spirit was convicting me, and He follows up conviction with correction, not condemnation.

Tears fell from my eyes one morning when I heard God say, "You hurt My child." But He followed that with, "If you use tough love, still express your love." The Lord followed up His convicting truth with corrective instruction, and that was comforting to me. Now I knew what to do going forward should I ever need to use tough love again. (I used tough love with my dad for several months during the last year of his life. He struggled with drug addiction.) Now I know that tough love must include letting the loved one know that even though I'm intentionally making them uncomfortable, I do love them, and that's the reason I'm making them uncomfortable.

"I forgive you and I will always love you more than you can understand," the Lord reminded me constantly.

Another name for the Holy Spirit is Comforter. He comforts us with the truth.

Counsel

God counsels us with His wisdom, giving us insight for decision making. It's incredible to receive privileged information from the one who created and operates the universe. Colossians 2:3 says that all the treasures of wisdom and knowledge are hidden in Christ. Knowing that all the wisdom I need for deciding is available to me because the Spirit of Christ lives in me is an immense confidence builder. The key is remembering that God and all His wisdom is available to me, within my heart.

Guidance

There are times when all we need is to know what God wants us to do. We need His guidance. We operate within space and time limitations, but God doesn't. He knows what tomorrow holds as well as all the factors of current situations. As we're trying to navigate through life's decisions, big and small, we need to remember that a word from God is all we need. Often, just being aware of Him brings that much-needed guidance.

Personal Application

- Are you aware of God's presence and involvement in your current circumstances?

- What is He saying and doing in your current situation?

―3―

Invoke

To invoke God is the expression of brilliant faith.

I knocked on the back door of the well-kept old farmhouse at the edge of the county. A small, pleasant, smartly dressed lady in her fifties opened the door and asked if she could help me.

I gave her my pat introduction. "Hey, I'm Gabriel Tew. I'm with the county, updating our information on all the real estate property for tax purposes. May I ask you a few questions?"

"Sure."

I went through my list, and she gave me the answers. Then I asked if she minded if I took measurements of the outside of the house.

"Have you ever heard of a Christian magazine called *Voice*?" she asked, ignoring my question.

"No, ma'am," I answered, surprised by her random response. "I'm a Christian, but I've never heard of that magazine."

"You know," she said, "if there's something between you and someone, all you have to do is go to that person and talk with them, and God will work it out for you."

―•―

At that time, my dad and I were butting heads like never before, and that's saying something. I had just graduated from

17

college and come back home to work on the family farm one last summer before moving on with my life. At the end of long, hard workdays, I would ride my bike several miles, training for a trip across the country a friend and I were planning. My dad thought that was stupid. College was over, and it was time to succeed in a career, not in pedaling a bicycle. In my mind, he didn't get me at all, so I tried to ignore him, which came across as disrespectful. Tension thickened between us, and we clashed at every opportunity.

Finally, one day I'd had enough. I was doing him a favor working on the farm that summer anyway, so I left after a harsh exchange between the two of us. I got a job with the county tax department, moved into an apartment in town, and we barely spoke to one another for five months—only at Thanksgiving and Christmas family gatherings, and even then with as few words as possible.

To worsen matters, instead of turning to the Lord in this crisis, I turned back to my old lifestyle. I resumed my use of alcohol and drugs and took on the values, desires, and behavior I'd had more than a year and a half earlier before I surrendered my life to Christ. I was daily emptying myself of the life Jesus had poured into me and filling myself with the emptiness of satisfying my fleshly desires.

During this time of pushing God aside in favor of my selfish desires, I knew this lifestyle had to be temporary for me. I knew it wasn't who I was, and the longer I stayed out of fellowship with the Lord, the more miserable I became. I knew the time would come when I would repent and turn back to Him. I remember once, around that time, sitting in a circle with party friends passing around a joint, all of us talking about what we'd be doing in the upcoming year. Everyone told about their plans for jobs, school, or whatever. Then someone asked what my plans were.

"I'm gonna get back right with the Lord," I responded honestly and without much thought.

The friend who asked the question looked at me and nodded, like he agreed that was the right thing for me to do. That was our last time spent together.

A few days after that, I'd had enough. It was time for me to repent and to turn to God as I should've done months before, instead of turning away from Him. Before going to bed that night, I got down on my knees beside my bed. It was time to pray, time to recommit my life to Jesus. As I opened my mouth, though, nothing would come out. I was unable to formulate any words in my mind to express to the Lord. I had nothing. I was empty. I saw that I was even further from Him than I'd thought I was, and that was alarming. How was I going to get back to Him? Was it even possible? Had my treatment of Him forever closed the door on our relationship?

In desperation I uttered from the depths of my heart the only two words I had: "Help me!"

Without any confidence in that prayer, I went to bed and didn't really think about it again. A few days later, just going about doing my job, I knocked on the back door of a well-kept old farmhouse at the edge of the county.

"If there's something between you and someone, all you have to do is go to that person and talk with them, and God will work it out for you," she had said.

I was jolted, because I knew God was speaking through this little lady into a hidden and neglected part of my heart. I was glad to be wearing sunglasses because I felt my eyes filling up, and I pushed back as hard as I could against the emotion.

Finally, though, I lost the battle and a tear spilled over and rolled down my face. As it came down from behind my sunglasses, she saw it and visibly reacted as if she knew she had captured me.

"Would you like to come inside and let me pray for you?" I nodded, unable to speak.

She told me her name (Miss Doris), took me into her living room, placed a chair in the center of the room, and asked me to sit in it. I sat in the chair and she on the couch, and she began to talk to me. She told me she spent her days taking care of her elderly incontinent father in that old farmhouse. Her tone was one of submission and obedience to God's assignment for her. I had the feeling she felt tucked away from the life she would've chosen in favor of serving her dad and her heavenly Father. I didn't get it at the time, but she was letting me know that God had led me into her obscure-seeming life, and that He was about to bring immense joy to both of us. And He was.

She rose from the couch, placed her hands on my head, and began praying for me. I don't remember what she prayed, but I do remember that as she prayed, she became increasingly excited. It was as if she could see God doing what she was asking Him to do as she asked Him to do it. She would even laugh at times out of sheer joy over what she knew God was doing in me. She prayed, giggled, and became so excited that she began dancing and lifting her hands in praise to God. As all this was happening, I felt the Spirit of God moving in me and lifting off my shoulders a burden I'd been unknowingly carrying for a long time.

After praying and praising God for a half hour, Miss Doris, exhausted but still excited, stopped. I'd been set free. Feeling as light as a feather, I thanked her profusely. She offered me a glass of tea, and we talked a few minutes more. Finally, my job required that I move on, but I drove out of her driveway completely different from when I drove in.

The first evidence of the Spirit's miraculous work in me, other than my sense of freedom and joy, came as I drove onto the road as I left Miss Doris' house. Out of pure habit, I stuck a pinch of smokeless tobacco inside my lower lip. Before I went a hundred feet further, however, I was pulling over onto the shoulder of the road. That dip of tobacco, something I could hardly live without before, was now so disgusting to me that I had to get it out of my mouth. I opened my door and spit it out on the ground. It was then that I remembered my two-word prayer to God a few nights before.

———•———

Invoke means "to call upon with earnest desire or to call out to for help." Since Jesus issued the invitation to ask for what we need in His name, invoking Him is a natural part of our faith in Him. Faith without invoking God is faith unexpressed. Faith is meant to be not only possessed but also expressed.

> Faith is meant to be not only possessed but also expressed.

———•———

Besides the inexplicable joy and being set free from a nicotine habit, the Lord continued to help me in several miraculous ways. I did talk to my dad. The Lord led me to apologize to him, and our relationship recovered from the damage of the previous summer and the ensuing silence. God also turned around completely and victoriously a situation with a guy with whom I had been at great odds. When I told him about my experience of God helping me in such a miraculous way when I asked Him, this guy was surprisingly interested, and he surrendered his life to Jesus. I was so excited at what God was doing that I went back to give Miss Doris the good report.

After listening to my testimony and sharing in my excitement, Miss Doris again took our conversation into a random direction.

"If you ask God for the qualities you want in a wife, He will answer your prayer," she said.

"I don't need to do that, Miss Doris. I already know the girl I want to marry."

I did call on the Lord for help in making that girl my wife, and He did help me, but that's another story for another chapter in another book. The life of brilliant faith is a life of invoking the Lord again and again.

Personal Application

- Recall a time when you invoked the Lord and how He responded.

–4–

Trust

To trust God is the essence of brilliant faith.

Everything about faith comes down to trust. Of all the single words we could use to define faith, trust defines it best. We could say that trust is the verb for the noun faith. If we want to measure our faith, look no further; the way we trust reflects our faith.

Our salvation begins when we decide to trust Jesus Christ to forgive our sins and adopt us into His family forever. Every part of brilliant faith includes trust. We trust God's Word as we become familiar with Him. We are aware of Him in our situation because we trust that He is with us. We invoke Him, trusting that He hears us and will respond to us. When we heed the Lord (We haven't reached that chapter yet, but you'll soon see), we trust Him through that process. Trust is the most important faith word, and we need to understand what it looks like.

What Trust Looks Like

In Matthew 17:20, Jesus used the analogy of a seed to describe faith. A seed is small but yields something gi-

> Trust is the most important faith word, and we need to understand what it looks like.

gantic. It is hidden and can't be seen in the soil, but what it produces is spectacular. Trust germinates in the heart. Its beginnings may not be visible, but it eventually manifests something magnificent. If you have faith the size of a mustard seed, you can move mountains and transplant trees from dry land into the sea (Luke 17:5-6). Trust produces evidence of itself.

> *If your brother sins against you, rebuke him; and if he repents, forgive him. And if he sins against you seven times in a day, and seven times in a day returns to you, saying, "I repent," you shall forgive him* (Luke 17:3-4).

Jesus' disciples had trouble seeing themselves as able to do what Jesus had just commanded: forgive your brother as often as he asks you to, even if it's seven times every day. They recognized their lack of faith was limiting them, so they asked Jesus to increase it.

> *And the apostles said to the Lord, "'increase our faith." So the Lord said, "If you have faith as a mustard seed, you can say to this mulberry tree, 'Be pulled up by the roots and be planted in the sea,' and it would obey you"* (Luke 17:5-6).

I'm not sure how they expected Him to increase their faith. Maybe they thought He would lay hands on them or somehow impart greater faith to them in a mystical way. He responded by painting a picture of what it looks like to trust God's power. He knew the way to increase their faith was to show them what trust looks like.

Trust is like a tree. Its many parts manifests through a process. The process starts with a planted seed, then begins to form the root, then the trunk, the limbs, leaves, and flowers, and finally, the fruit.

The Fruit of Trust

1. Commitment

The only trust that doesn't manifest e~
tical trust. Real trust always does. D. Jan
people understand this by placing a chair o~
ing, "Do you believe that chair can hold you.

The answer is always, "Yes."

"You may believe it will, but you aren't trusting it until you sit in it. Will you please sit in the chair?"

Then the person sits in the chair and understands the difference (*Evangelism Explosion*, Vol 4 p.34).

The correlation is that we can say we believe Jesus died on the cross to purchase our freedom from eternal damnation, but we don't really trust God's forgiveness until we commit our lives to Him. We're not going to commit to something we don't trust. Commitment is the first fruit of trust.

The word "commit" provides a clear illustration of what it means to trust. *Com* means "together with" and *mit* means "send or put." The word picture is putting something together with something else. When we mail a letter, we are putting it into the hands of the postal service, trusting that they will deliver it.

When a man proposes to a woman and she says yes, she is putting her future together with his, and he is putting his with hers; they are committing and trusting their future to one another. When individuals trust Christ Jesus, they are putting their lives forever with His, fully committing and trusting Him in every way. A picture of commitment is a picture of trusting.

Around five thousand years ago, humankind so displeased God that He prepared to destroy them and the earth with a great flood. Noah found favor in God's eyes, and the Lord in-

d him to build an enormous boat that would perpetuate
beyond the flood (Gen. 6:1-14). In the earth's history,
throughout the lifetimes of all Noah's ancestors, it had never
rained. A global flood was as new a concept to Noah's generation as an intergalactic war would be to ours. Yet Noah's response was one of trust. "So Noah did everything exactly as
God had commanded him" (Gen. 6:22 NLT).

Consider the backdrop of Noah's encounter with God.
God warned Noah that a previously unknown phenomenon
was coming. The culture of Noah's day consisted of people
whose thoughts were constantly and completely evil (Gen.
6:5). The task the Lord assigned to Noah was so monumental
that it would take decades to complete. Yet, despite what
could've been discouraging factors, Noah committed himself
to do what God instructed him to do. He trusted the Lord and
bore the first fruit of that trust: commitment.

2. Patience

Whenever extended time is factored into a challenge, the
need for patience becomes greater. Intensify the difficulty and
we need patience even more. Subtract patience from the equa-
tion and we fold, forfeiting our prize. Patience is not only a
virtue, it's also of immense value. James put the concept of extended trials into perspective for us.

> *My friends, consider yourselves fortunate when all kinds of trials
> come your way, for you know that when your faith succeeds in
> facing such trials, the result is the ability to endure. Make sure
> that your endurance carries you all the way without failing, so
> that you may be perfect and complete, lacking nothing* (James
> 1:2-4 GNT).

When our faith succeeds—when we continue trusting all

the way through a trial—we have strengthened our patience. Strong patience enables us to continue our faith all the way through our lives. Even though our faith is being tested in the trial, both our faith and our patience are becoming stronger.

Being patient is simply not quitting. There's a poem I once heard, and I've used it many times as a simple tool to remind myself and others not to give up. The first stanza goes like this:

Plow on, plow on, plow on, plow on Plow on, plow on, plow on, plow on.
The second stanza says:
Plow on, plow on, plow on, plow on Plow on, plow on, plow on, plow on.
The third stanza goes:
Plow on, plow on, plow on, plow on Plow on, plow on, plow on, plow on.

People always laugh because of the redundancy, but it's repetitive because patience is simple: just keep going; don't quit, just plow on.

It takes trust to continue. Trust that God will give us the strength. Trust that it'll be worth it. Trust that circumstances won't defeat us. Trust that God will meet the need, whatever that is, from one situation to another. Trusting God must be open-ended. If it expires before God completes His work, we may miss out.

The Bible doesn't detail the challenges Noah faced, but we know he had to build a boat larger than the *Titanic* with primitive technology. It took him considerable time to build it. I'm sure he had multiple temptations to quit, but he had just as many opportunities to continue. Whatever the circumstances were,

Noah continued trusting. In the process, he built an ark, his faith, and his patience. Trust is vital, and its second fruit is patience.

3. Miracle

God brought all the animals needed to preserve their species to the ark. He caused rain to fall from the sky for forty days and nights straight. He caused fountains of water from underneath the ground to break through the earth's surface. The waters covered the entire planet, even the mountaintops. Once the water subsided, Noah and his family were safe, the only people left alive on the earth. God performed numerous miracles as Noah trusted Him.

The Lord performs countless more miracles than we know about. Every time a person trusts Jesus for salvation, the Lord gives that person His Spirit; that's a miracle. Every time the Holy Spirit interprets God's Word so someone can understand it. Every time He guides someone with a nudge or a gentle whisper. Every time God deploys His angel armies to fight hellish forces working to destroy His children. Every time God works to affect our situations. All those times are miracles.

King Solomon wrote, "Trust in the Lord with all your heart, and lean not to your own understanding. In all your ways acknowledge Him, and He will direct your paths" (Prov. 3:5-6). Our trust must extend beyond our understanding. God certainly isn't going to limit His work to what we can understand. How disappointing would that be? When we trust Him without requiring understanding of everything, we set ourselves up for pleasant surprises. And God never runs out of surprises. They are His miracles.

"The condition for a miracle is difficulty, however the condition for a great miracle is not difficulty, but impossibility" (Angus Buchan).

Personal Application

- Are you trusting God to forgive your sins and give you eternal life?

- What else are you trusting Him for?

−5−

Heed

To heed God is to walk out brilliant faith.

Only he who believes is obedient and only he who is obedient believes. − *Dietrich Bonhoeffer*

Several weeks after our annual church retreat, Sidney, our oldest son, seventeen at the time, told us he had surrendered his life to Jesus at the retreat. On the last night of the retreat, he and our incredibly good friend, CJ Blankenship, had sat by the fire talking until dawn. Before the other campers began to stir, Sidney made the decision to put his faith in Christ. He said it brought him such joy and freedom that he took off running and ran until he collapsed. Sharlene and I were overjoyed at this best-ever news! The only question we had was why he hadn't told us about it sooner.

"I wanted to walk it out for a little while before I told you," he said.

I understood and respected that. He wanted to exercise his faith with his life before he professed it with his mouth. Nothing is wrong with someone not professing their faith immediately. Jesus told some people not to tell anyone about the miracles He had performed for them, and to others to go tell people what He had done, each depending on the circumstances. Sidney wanted to practice his faith before reporting it. For that reason, he took some time to heed the Lord.

Heed isn't a word we use every day, so a definition is in order. In the sense I'm using it here, heed means "to observe God and respond appropriately to Him." Like the other components of brilliant faith, heeding has its own role, but it's also present in each of the other components. We use the observe-respond process to become familiar with God, to be aware of Him in our situations, to invoke Him, and when we trust Him.

James 2:26 says, "Faith without works is dead." To translate that into the brilliant faith language: FAITH without works is just FAIT. It has no H. There is no heeding. Faith in God that doesn't heed God and what God says is missing something. It isn't complete. While it's true that faith without works is dead, it's also true that works without faith are dead. Without faith, good works will not save us. Paul spent much of his ministry clarifying that God's grace saves us by faith alone. While works are a vital part of faith, they do not save us apart from faith. (More on that in Chapter 11.)

Heeding God is like the hands and feet of our faith. If we cut them off, our faith doesn't function properly nor accomplish much. We must view heeding God not as apart from faith, but as a vital part of faith.

> **We must view heeding God not as apart from faith, but as a vital part of faith.**

Observe

The restaurants I frequent have one server taking care of several tables. The finer the restaurant, the better the server-to-patron ratio. I once had dinner at a restaurant that designated one server for each table. Our party of six received first-rate service for that dinner.

In some settings, several servants are assigned to one person. Historically, when a wealthy monarch dined, one servant was responsible for his drink, another to remove items from his table, another to keep his table free of the slightest crumbs, and others for other parts of his meal. The ratio could be twenty to one, as opposed to the one to twenty I'm used to. When servants tend to a king, they are keen to watch his every move, even his slightest gestures, to sense every need or desire he might have.

Heeding carries that kind of vigilance and sensitivity to God, our King. Because we know and trust Him, we want to please Him. We study His every move, hoping to notice a movement or sound that signals a desire from Him. The more familiar we are with Him, the greater our interest in heeding Him.

Dogs can hear sounds from at least four times farther away than humans can. They can also hear nearly twice the range of frequencies that humans can hear. Faith gives our spiritual ears such an advantage in hearing God. On at least three occasions Jesus said, "He who has ears to hear, let him hear" (Matt. 11:15; 13:9, 43).

Besides God opening them up for us, our "ears to hear" flow from our passioned interest in knowing Him, hearing Him, and pleasing Him. Sharlene and I have six kids. Now that they're all grown, no two of them live in the same state. But Sharlene and I love them as much as ever, and we're interested in knowing anything that's going on in their lives. We track them through social media, and we text and talk with them as often as possible by phone or video chat. We try to give them their space, but it's hard. We care about them as much as when their bedrooms were down the hall from ours, and we pay attention to them as closely as we can. Likewise, when we honestly love God in our hearts, our interest in Him compels us into a position to hear His voice. Observing God takes effort, but it's also a natural part of brilliant faith.

Respond

Under Old Testament law, there were two ways to respond appropriately to God. One was by obeying His prescribed laws, and the other was by freewill offerings and actions. In Christ, those same two types of response to Him exist for us.

The pinnacle of the law in the Old Testament was to love and serve God without revering any other idols or gods. The only appropriate response to that requirement was to strictly obey it. Since Jesus fulfilled all the requirements of the law and sacrificed Himself to pay our sin-debt, the only appropriate response for us is to put our faith in Him. With our faith in Him, we have God's Spirit living within us and the Bible available to us; our appropriate response to God's direction is obedience.

As we walk out life in Christ, we walk with immeasurable freedom to respond to Him with ideas we birth in our own hearts. Authoring this book is my response to a desire I sense that God has for people to understand faith—that it really is brilliant faith. This isn't something the Lord instructed me to do. I'm asking Him to direct me in every word of it, but it's my freewill offering to Him. I hope He finds it acceptable and uses it to help people know and trust Him more.

Fruit of FAITH

Heeding is the fruit of brilliant faith. Fruit has three purposes:

1. Identity—It identifies the plant.

2. Food—It benefits others.

3. Seed—It reproduces.

Works alone is different from heeding. Heeding is the fruit of brilliant faith. Works that don't stem from faith are like chemically produced foods: they serve only as food, often unhealthy food, but they don't carry the identity or the seed.

Jesus said all people would identify His followers by our love for each other (John 16:35) and by how we treat those in need (Heb. 13:6). Those are outward products of our faith. They are our fruit. We are known by our fruit, identified by our heeding.

As we observe and respond to the Lord, we will do things that benefit other people. We'll be generous with our resources, caring with acts of service, encouraging with our words, and exemplary with our lifestyle. Our heeding will be food, or benefits, for people to enjoy.

As we heed God, people see that we are His and benefit from what we say and do, which makes them hungry for what we have—Jesus. The fruit of our faith, heeding, reproduces in others the faith that reconciles us with God and gives us eternal life.

Personal Application

- What is God saying to you that requires an appropriate response from you?

- In what way have you responded to God?

Section 2

Brilliant Faith in Scripture

Since FAITH is God's chosen vehicle through which we understand and relate to Him, the Bible obviously has much to say about the subject. This section deals with nine important brilliant faith themes that are present in Scripture. These nine chapters will help you:

- See your faith as something tangible.

- Learn to grow your faith.

- Understand the seed-like power your faith has.

- Learn to overcome worry, doubt, fear, and confusion with your faith.

- Understand what kind of faith impressed Jesus.

- Have the most important kind of faith you can have.

- Use your faith for protection against the enemy.

- Become consistent with your faith.

- Know the two seasonings that must always accompany your faith.

6

Substance and Evidence

In God's Kingdom, our faith is concrete proof of our citizenship.

Now Faith is the substance of things hoped for, the evidence of things not seen (Heb. 11:1).

Hebrews 11 is commonly called the Hall of Faith, because it lists people in biblical history whose faith accomplished significant exploits. The chapter begins by naming two roles in which faith serves. "Now faith is the substance of things hoped for, the evidence of things not seen" (Heb. 11:1). Faith serves as substance and as evidence. I'm so glad this verse is in the Bible because seeing faith in these two roles helps us understand how valuable it is.

Substance

Heaven sees our faith altogether differently from the way earth does. God and His heavenly subjects see it as tangible and real, as a substance. Substance means "stand under." A lot can rest upon our faith when we are deeply and broadly familiar with God. As Hebrews 11:1 tells us, our hope rests upon our faith. Our faith is the substance upon which it rests, and brilliant faith is strong enough that we never have to lose our hope.

Hope, in the biblical sense, has three components:

• It's for something in the future.

- It's for something we desire.

- It's for certain.

When we use the word *hope* in modern everyday English, it's for something in the future, and it's for something we desire. But it's not for certain. We really want it to become reality, but it may or may not. We hope our team wins, we hope traffic isn't bad, or we hope we get a good grade on our test. None of those things are sure. The hope we have in Jesus, however, is certain.

God has made promises to those whose faith is in Him about things in the future. Here are a few of them:

- There will be a new creation, and we'll live in a new city with Jesus (Rev. 21:1-4).

- When our life on earth is over, those with faith in Jesus will be with Him (2 Cor. 5:8).

- God will wipe away our tears (Rev. 7:17).

- We'll have no more pain (Rev. 21:4).

- Our enemy will no longer be present to deceive and tempt us (Rev. 20:10).

- We will have no need for a sun or moon because the Lord God will be the light (Rev. 21:23).

We have certainty of those future things because of our faith. We are familiar with God's promises. When we're going through a tough time and circumstances threaten our joy, we remember those promises. Being aware of how they relate to our current situation gives us strength to continue through our troubles. Hope has the power to get us through our struggles because it keeps our eyes on the prize we'll receive at the end. The way we maintain our hope is through our faith.

Evidence

A heavenly kingdom exists in the hearts of Jesus-believers and in the air, where the angels of God's army war against the angels of Satan. God is moving in Spirit form throughout the earth, through all of space and in the deepest chasms of the souls of people, transforming everything He touches. People are standing in the favor of God, as if under a beam of light coming from heaven, their hearts filled with joy, peace, love, and gratitude because they are His.

Though we can't see these things, they are proven by brilliant faith. God's kingdom has a completely different view of us and our faith than the world does. The world usually sees only the outcome of our faith, not the faith itself. But God knows our hearts and therefore, our faith itself. He doesn't need to wait to see what our faith will produce. As we walk with God and become more familiar with Him, we grow in our ability to discern faith. When we can discern faith, not just its results, it serves as evidence of things unseen.

For the last couple of years in the 1990s and the first couple of years of the 2000s, I was on staff as associate pastor at Gospel Tabernacle in Dunn, North Carolina. One Sunday we had planned a big community outreach event on our church campus. We rented rides and set up booths for games and food, like a county fair (except it was all free). We invited the entire community to the event, and scores of church members worked as volunteers, all for the purpose of showing our community that we loved them, and Jesus loved them. We set up chairs and a stage where our band would play and share the good news of Jesus. We put a lot of work into it, and our team of volunteers and the entire church were pumped about the event. As we watched the weather forecast all day Saturday and Sunday morning, though, we prepared ourselves for a rainy Sunday afternoon.

That was a special Sunday. Not only had we planned the outreach event, but we also had a guest speaker for the morning worship service, U.S. Army General Jerry Boykin. General Boykin had commanded numerous high-profile missions and is highly decorated. He is also an ordained minister who preached about Jesus, once getting himself into some trouble because he preached while in his Army uniform. Our church was standing-room-only with many people coming to hear what General Boykin had to say.

After a time of worshiping the Lord with music and before General Boykin spoke, our lead pastor, Ron Wooten, walked up to the podium and began to share the inclement weather plan with the congregation.

"We're going to move this afternoon's event into the family life center. We won't be able to have our rides, but we'll move as many of our booths as possible inside. At least we'll still be able to—"

He stopped midsentence, clinched his eyes shut, shook his head violently and began to pound his fist on the podium. "No! No! No! NO! That's not what we're going to do! We're going to have our event today! And we're going to have it outside! It will not rain until we're done with our event, in the name of Jesus! We're going forward as planned and the rain will hold off, in Jesus' name!" Having made this declaration, Ron sat down. The congregation sat with blank stares. Nobody reacted. We were all nervous.

What was Ron doing? What if he's wrong? What if it rains us out and makes us look like fools?

While everyone was processing what Ron had just done, one of the men in the church introduced General Boykin. General Boykin walked onto the stage and to the podium.

"Where did you get this guy?!" he asked, looking over at Ron in amazement.

General Boykin recognized Ron's faith. Most people in the room didn't know whether it was faith or foolishness. But the General, we would find out moments later, knew a thing or two about faith. His stories of the miracles he witnessed and experienced after calling out to the Lord as commander on his Delta Force missions were nothing short of amazing. To him, Ron's bold proclamation was evidence—evidence of things unseen.

Everyone else got to see the evidence a few hours later. We held our event outside—without a drop of rain. Hundreds of people were enjoying the rides, games, and food. At the planned time, we gathered everyone to hear about the love of God. People placed their trust in Jesus that day. Then we broke down the equipment and brought it inside. The moment we brought everything in, the sky opened and dumped the forecasted rain, just a few hours later than forecasted.

Ron's faith that day was evidence of things happening that we couldn't see. He was familiar with Jesus' promise that our faith could move mountains, including the account of Jesus calming a storm by speaking to it. He was familiar with Jesus' statement to His disciples that they, and we, would do greater things than He did because of the Holy Spirit's presence in us. Ron was aware that the Holy Spirit was with us, that our event was to promote Jesus, and that what we bound or loosed on the earth would be bound or loosed in heaven. He invoked God, speaking in the name of Jesus. He led us forward, trusting that God would hold off the rain. He continued in close communion with God that afternoon, seeking Him, willing to do whatever He directed him to do—heeding God. It was a glorious day of seeing God work according to someone's daring faith. But it didn't stop there.

A couple of years later, I led a team to birth a church in Wilmington, North Carolina. Our church, Grace Harbor Church, had a strong outreach focus. We adopted one of the housing projects in the inner city and held monthly outdoor events there during the warm months. The events were like the one Gospel Tabernacle held that day, but on a smaller scale.

One day our event was threatened by a forecast of close to 100 percent chance of rain. but I knew what to do. I stood before the people in our church and boldly proclaimed that it wasn't going to rain. We had kingdom work to do in people's lives, and the Lord would hold off the rain in the name of Jesus! When it came time for the event, there was no rain. When we finished the event and got everything loaded, it began to rain.

This happened four separate times in Wilmington. Then there was a fifth time. This time my faith was lacking. I told our outreach team that we were cancelling the event due to rain. Later that afternoon, at the time the event was scheduled to begin, the rain stopped, the clouds parted, and the sun shone brightly. Then at the time the event would've ended, the clouds returned, and the rain resumed. The Lord was saying so clearly to me, "See what I'm willing to do if you'll just believe?"

The kingdom of heaven was at work that day, doing things unseen. My faith was missing, though, so I showed no evidence that unseen things were at work. The other four times, I had faith as Ron had. Our faith showed evidence on those days that events were happening that couldn't be seen. God was working in all those situations, but only when we had faith was there evidence that He was working. Brilliant faith is evidence of things unseen.

Jesus died to cancel our sin-debt. He rose from the grave. He ascended to heaven. The Holy Spirit has been poured out into the hearts of believers. The kingdom of heaven is active all the time. All those statements are true whether we have faith or not. When we do have faith, however, it serves as evidence that they are true. Our brilliant faith is evidence to us that we have eternal life, and it's evidence for others that they can have eternal life too.

Personal Application

- What unseen things in your life are evidenced by your faith?

- What do you know about God that causes your faith to be substance and evidence?

- What awareness do you have of God being present and involved that strengthens your faith to be substance and evidence?

-7-

Comes and Grows

Brilliant faith comes when we understand God's Word.
It grows as our understanding grows.

How is brilliant faith birthed in us? How does it grow? The answer to both questions is the same: by God's Word. I use two primary passages of Scripture in this chapter to explain how faith comes and how it grows.

Coming

Paul wrote to the church in Rome: "Faith comes by hearing, and hearing by the word of God" (Rom. 10:17). In that context, the word *hearing* means "understanding and hearing." The figurative meaning is like the way Jesus used the word hear when He said, "He who has ears to hear let him hear" (Mark 4:9). He didn't mean it in a literal sense, that people who had ears on the sides of their heads should receive the sound waves as He spoke to them. He meant that people who have a desire to understand and a soft, humble heart toward the Lord should really listen and understand what He was saying.

Paul's meaning is that faith comes when we understand the truth, which comes from God's Word. Specifically, he was addressing the need for people to take the good-news message of Jesus Christ to people who hadn't heard of Him. When they did that, the people would understand who Jesus is and could choose to place their faith in Him.

Paul's statement also has a further application, a more general one. When people hear or read God's Word, if they have a desire to understand and a soft, humble heart toward the Lord, they will gain an understanding of it with the Holy Spirit's help. As we gain that understanding, we can choose faith.

The condition of our heart is the key. Consider this. The disciples were in a boat rowing against the wind when Jesus came walking by on the water. They were afraid and called out to Him. He soon got into the boat with them, and the wind stopped immediately. "[The disciples] were greatly amazed in themselves beyond measure, and marveled. For they had not understood about the loaves, because their heart was hardened" (Mark 6:51-52). They acted as if this revealed afresh for them who Jesus was, despite all His previous teaching and miracles, including the most recent one of miraculously feeding the multitude. The reason they were so overly amazed is because their hearts were hardened, because they somehow didn't understand the miracle Jesus had just performed earlier that day when He fed more than five thousand people with five loaves and two fish. They ended up with twelve baskets of leftovers, but their hearts were hardened.

Think about that. They didn't understand the miracle of the loaves. Somehow, they didn't grasp that since Jesus had demonstrated His incredible power and compassion in that miracle, they need not fear a storm nor be surprised when He miraculously calmed it. If they had understood that Jesus would take care of His followers, their hearts would've softened toward Him. When they saw Him on the water, they would've recognized Him. When He calmed the wind, they would've recognized it as normal for Him. Impressive? Yes! But for Him, normal.

The condition of our heart is critical. The four Gospels are replete with people who saw Jesus work miracles but because their hearts were hardened against Him, they missed their opportunity for faith. Likewise, the past twenty centuries have been dark-stained by the multitudes who have heard God's Word but because of the hardness of their hearts, missed faith.

However, many people in those same twenty centuries have chosen faith. Men, women, and children on all seven continents have chosen faith because they gained understanding of God's Word with hungry and soft hearts. I'm one of those people whose heart was softened, making it easy for me to choose faith.

In October 1983, I was asleep in my college dorm room. I awoke around 3:00 a.m. and saw a demonic spirit moving along the wall, making its way to my bed. Once there, it descended upon me, and I became unable to move or speak. I was so terrified that I could barely breathe. Suddenly, I remembered what I'd heard my friend, Cliff, say just a few days before.

Cliff was one of my best friends, and he had given his life to Jesus a few months before. The change in him was drastic. Real joy had replaced the surface happiness he had previously manufactured with drugs and alcohol. I was still in the futility of those pursuits, and Cliff now stood out like a light amid the darkness of my life. The words he spoke, as he talked about God, were genuine and different; they were words of life.

In what felt like a battle for my very life, I remembered something Cliff had said: "At the name of Jesus, a demon has to flee."

Like a lifeline thrown to me, the memory of that statement landed in my mind; in desperation, I latched onto it.

"Jesus," I mouthed, unable to even whisper. Immediately, I sensed strength rising in me and my assailant weakening.

Then I was able to whisper, "Jesus."

More strength came.

Then I could speak, "Jesus."

The demon was losing its hold on me.

"Jesus!" I shouted, "Jesus! Jesus! Jesus!"

The deadly spirit lifted off me and disappeared through the wall.

I was amazed at what I had just experienced. Merely speaking the name Jesus had saved me from a demonic attack. About twenty hours later, in a prayer meeting in another dorm room, I put my trust in Christ to save my soul from an eternity of demons like the one I had fought that night. That experience humbled me, softened my heart, and made me hungry for more of Jesus.

I heard one truth spoken by my friend. It wasn't a scriptural quote, but it was a scriptural truth. The Gospels record that Jesus cast out many demons, and He commanded the devil to leave Him in the wilderness. The devil obeyed, leaving no question that Jesus had authority over him.

Jesus dealt the final blows to Satan when He freed us from sin by His death on the cross and His resurrection from the grave. James 4:7 says, "Resist the devil and he will flee from you." What better way to resist him than with the name of the one who has already defeated him? Also, Paul demanded "in the name of Jesus" that a demon, who was speaking through a Philippian slave girl, come out of her, and it did (Acts 16:16-18). Years later, from a prison in Rome, Paul wrote a letter to the church located in Philippi, the very city where he had cast out that demon. The letter said:

> God also has highly exalted [Jesus] *and given Him the name which is above every name, that at the name of Jesus every knee should bow, of those in heaven, and of those on earth, and of those under the earth, and that every tongue should confess that Jesus Christ is Lord* (Phil. 2:9-11).

I heard the Word of God. I understood it well enough to heed it, and it saved me. If you ever find yourself under the attack of demonic forces, trust the power of Jesus and speak His name against those forces. You'll be amazed at the power of His mere name. If you haven't trusted in that name to save you into eternal life, I hope you'll call on Him—even now—whose name is Jesus, the Savior.

Growing

"Increase our faith!" the disciples implored Jesus (Luke 17:5). They were responding to a requirement He had just established for them. "If your brother sins, rebuke him, and if he repents, forgive him. If he sins against you seven times in a day, and seven times comes back to you and says, 'I repent,' forgive him" (Luke 17:3-4).

They had been with Jesus long enough to recognize that faith would be required to forgive so patiently, and they wanted more of it. Jesus said, "If you have faith as small as a mustard seed, you can say to this mulberry tree, 'Be uprooted and planted in the sea,' and it will obey you" (Luke 17:6).

Jesus' response to their request for more faith reveals two instructions we too need to understand.

First, don't think of faith as the thing that's big. Rather, realize that what faith produces is big.

47

Faith itself is small, like a seed, and our part is to sow our seed. But it's God who does the big work. He gives the increase. He moves the trees and the mountains. We sow our seed of faith in Jesus, and He does the magnificent work of saving us from what we deserve and giving us what we most need—eternal life.

The second instruction we need to understand from Jesus' response is this: once you've done remarkable things with your faith, remember that you're still God's servant. Suppose you had a servant plowing or looking after the sheep. Would you say to the servant when he comes in from the field, "Come along now and sit down to eat"? Would you not rather say, "Prepare my supper, get yourself ready and wait on me while I eat and drink; after that you may eat and drink"? Would you thank the servant because he did what he was told to do? So you also, when you have done everything you were told to do, should say, "We are unworthy servants; we have only done our duty" (See Luke 17:7-10 NIV).

We haven't earned anything with our faith. We've simply used what our Master has given us to do what He's called us to do. If we ever see ourselves as having accomplished what God has accomplished through us, our faulty perspective makes us bigger and God smaller. Anytime we have that attitude, we're headed for trouble. If our little faith seed produces miraculous results, we need to remember God was the one who did the heavy lifting. We simply did the small thing He asked us to do. We sowed our little seed. He's still God, and we're still His servants. Our role is to continue to serve our mighty God by faith.

Personal Application

- What message from God's Word has He used to add to your faith?

- Was there a time when you saw your seed of faith result in a miracle?

—8—

Seed

Brilliant faith is seed—it produces fruit like itself
but much greater than itself.

Jesus compared faith to seed. He said,

> *The kingdom of heaven is like a mustard seed, which a man took*
> *and sowed in his field, which indeed is the least of all the seeds;*
> *but when it is grown it is greater than the herbs and becomes a*
> *tree, so that the birds of the air come and nest in its branches*
> (Matt. 13:31-32).

If we want to grow something good in our lives, we need
the seed that has the information to produce good fruit. For
example, if someone wants to prosper in all things, they can
put their faith in Psalm 1:1-3:

> *Blessed is the man who walks not in the counsel of the ungodly,*
> *nor stands in the path of sinners, nor sits in the seat of the scorn-*
> *ful; but his delight is in the law of the Lord, and in His law he*
> *meditates day and night. He shall be like a tree planted by the*
> *rivers of water, that brings forth its fruit in its season, whose*
> *leaf also shall not wither; and whatever he does shall prosper.*

Those three verses expand our familiarity with God. They
tell us that He blesses the people who separate themselves
from the ungodly, the sinful, and the scornful; and He blesses
those who delight themselves in God's Word. Whoever does

this can expect a fruitful, prosperous life. That's some significant knowledge about God.

If someone would add that knowledge to the basis of their faith (Familiar), be sensitive to God's involvement in their life (Aware), call upon God when they so desire (Invoke), trust Him to be faithful to His promise (Trust), and stay in step with Him as He works in their life (Heed), brilliant faith will be at work in their life. Brilliant faith takes advantage of the opportunities found in God's Word, like Psalm 1:1-3, using it as a seed that produces something big. The last line in that passage contains the information needed to produce something great. It's just five words, "whatever he does shall prosper," and they have a general meaning.

If we analyze such a person's life, however, we see intimacy in their relationship with God; peace and love in their family relationships; respect and favor from people in their community; success in their professional and ministry endeavors; and consistent inner peace and joy, regardless of changes in circumstances. Each part of that blessed life is like a strong branch on which birds of the air can come and rest. What's more, that large tree came from a small seed of brilliant faith, a seed that contained the information needed to produce something so great.

Personal Application

- What Scripture can you sow as a seed of brilliant faith in your life?

—9—

Puny

Weak faith hinders our experiences with God.

The book of Matthew records four occasions on which Jesus told people their faith was puny.

You won't see the word *puny* as you read those passages in the Bible; instead, you'll see the word *little*. Strong's Concordance defines the Greek prefix attached to the word for faith as "puny." In each of those events, Jesus was letting them know they were missing a prize He was making available to them.

The prizes were four essential human needs: provision, protection, performance, and perception. We find them in Matthew chapters 6, 8, 14, and 16. Present in each case is the respective reason for their puny faith: worry (about provision), fear (for lack of protection), doubt (of ability to perform), and confusion (blocking perception). Let's analyze each case.

Provision

If we have strong faith, we'll trust God for the things we need, rather than worrying about them. That's what Jesus taught His disciples.

No one can serve two masters. For you will hate one and love the other; you will be devoted to one and despise the other. You cannot serve both God and money. That is why I tell you not to worry about everyday life—whether you have enough food and drink, or enough clothes to wear. Isn't life more than food, and your body more than clothing? Look at the birds. They don't plant or harvest or store food in barns, for your heavenly Father feeds them. And aren't you far more valuable to him than they are? Can all your worries add a single moment to your life? And why worry about your clothing? Look at the lilies of the field and how they grow. They don't work or make their clothing, yet Solomon in all his glory was not dressed as beautifully as they are. And if God cares so wonderfully for wildflowers that are here today and thrown into the fire tomorrow, he will certainly care for you. **Why do you have so little [puny] faith?** *So don't worry about these things, saying, 'What will we eat? What will we drink? What will we wear?' These things dominate the thoughts of unbelievers, but your heavenly Father already knows all your needs. Seek the Kingdom of God above all else, and live righteously, and he will give you everything you need"* (Matt. 6:24-33 NLT emphasis added).

It's simple logic. If God provides for the birds and the lilies, why would we worry about His provision for us? Only because our faith is puny. Here's what strong faith looks like in the case of provision:

- We are *familiar* with God's love for us and His promise to supply all our needs.
- We are more *aware* of His care for us than we are of our need.
- We *invoke* Him, presenting our request to Him.
- We *trust* that He will do what He said He would.
- We seek Him about what our role is in providing for our need and *heed* His instructions.

Paul wrote, "Don't fret or worry. Instead of worrying, pray. Let petitions and praises shape your worries into prayers, letting God know your concerns. Before you know it, a sense of God's wholeness, everything coming together for good, will come and settle you down. It's wonderful what happens when Christ displaces worry at the center of your life" (Phil. 4:6-7 MSG).

When we make our requests to God and give Him thanks, He replaces our worries with peace, which guards our hearts from worry's return. This process is a mystery, beyond our ability to understand. Our responsibility in it is to have faith.

Our faith doesn't carry the full load of our provision. Jesus didn't say it did. God is the one carrying that gigantic responsibility. The point Jesus made, and the one Paul made, is that strong faith will replace and prevent worrying and bring with it peace of mind. Puny faith won't do that. Brilliant faith will.

Protection

Matthew 8:23-27 finds Jesus and His disciples in a boat in the middle of the Sea of Galilee when a squall arose. The storm was so intense that the high waves were breaking into their boat, filling it with water, and the disciples feared for their lives.

They rushed to the hull of the boat where Jesus was sleeping and awoke Him with a question. "Don't you care that we're about to be killed?" Ignoring their question, Jesus posed one of His own, "Why are you so afraid, you puny-faiths?" Then He arose, spoke to the wind, "Peace! Be still!" and everything became calm.

The disciples needed protection from the life-threatening storm, but they were more aware of the storm than of Jesus' presence. Ignoring the most crucial factor in their situation was not logical: if Jesus were with them, they'd be okay. Sound logic would've led them to the assurance of their safety, but misdirected attention led them to irrational fear, which douses the flames of faith. Thus, Jesus' question, "Why are you so afraid?"

Our first son, Sidney, is a courageous young man. He is a graduate of The Citadel where he was the top Marine Corp cadet on campus his senior year. He's earned two black belts and enjoys living a little bit on the dangerous side. There was one day, though, when that wasn't the case.

When Sidney was twelve years old, we were at Sea World standing in line for a roller coaster ride. Somehow, he got it into his mind that we would die if we rode this rollercoaster, and he started freaking out.

His mother and I tried to reason with him. "Look at all these people in line. They're all willing to ride it. And think about all the people who have ridden this roller coaster. None of them have died or been injured. Why would anything happen to us?"

No matter how sound our logic, Sidney couldn't be convinced. He had somehow locked his focus onto the one-in-750 million chance that we would die on this ride. (I researched the odds of someone dying on a roller coaster.) We practically forced him to get on the ride. He ended up loving it and riding it repeatedly.

Faith in God is simple logic. The chance He'll be wrong or not follow through on His promise is far more favorable than one-in-750 million. It's zero. He's 100 percent dependable. However, if we get locked into focusing on circumstances that cause us to forget God, losing our awareness of Him, our faith becomes puny, and we can be dominated by fear. On the contrary, if we remain keenly aware of God, our confidence in Him will be strong and fear will have no place in our minds.

Performance

In Matthew 14 the disciples are on the water again. Jesus had just miraculously fed more than five-thousand people. He instructed His disciples to go ahead of Him across the Sea of Galilee while He sent the crowd home. Then He went up into the hills for time alone with the Father. Meanwhile, heavy winds blew in and violent waves were beating against the disciples' boat.

That's when Jesus came walking toward them on the water. They were terrified, thinking it was some sort of ghost, but Jesus called out to reassure them. Peter, displaying a courage that must have impressed his shipmates, shouted out for an invitation from Jesus to join Him on the water, which Jesus obliged.

Peter stepped out and began making his way to Jesus upon the water but soon distracted by the wind-whipped waves, he lost his Jesus-focus and began to sink.

"Save me!"

Jesus reached out and took his hand. "[Puny-faith], why did you doubt?"

If Peter were focused on Jesus—mindful of His presence, permission, and power—he knew he could perform a super-human, gravity-defying walk atop thin liquid, even as it churned around him. If he had continued without doubting and sinking and made it all the way to Jesus, I bet Jesus would've been impressed. I bet Peter's fellow disciples would've jumped out and joined them on the water. What a time they could've had, a memory and testimony they could've retold, the night they splashed and laughed out on the storm-tossed sea!

Once Peter shifted his attention away from Jesus and became enamored with the power of the winds, his tree-like faith was chopped down to a nubby stump. As a stump can't bear fruit, neither could Peter perform what Jesus called him to do. His awareness was of wind and waves, not of the water-walker. Doubt replaced belief. His faith was puny.

When we're trying to do something unusual or miraculous, something we know God has called us to do, we need to stay focused on Jesus. That's the secret to overcoming doubt and performing His will.

Perception

Matthew 16 reveals one of faith's surprising benefits.

Later, after they crossed to the other side of the lake, the disciples discovered they had forgotten to bring any bread. "Watch out!" Jesus warned them. "Beware of the yeast of the Pharisees and Sadducees."

At this they began to argue with each other because they hadn't brought any bread. Jesus knew what they were saying, so He said, "You have such [puny] faith! Why are you arguing with each other about having no bread? Don't you understand even yet? Don't you remember the five thousand I fed with five loaves, and the baskets of leftovers you picked up? Or the four thousand I fed with seven loaves, and the large baskets of leftovers you picked up? Why can't you understand that I'm not talking about bread? So again I say, 'Beware of the yeast of the Pharisees and Sadducees'" (Matt. 16:5-12 NLT).

Then at last they understood that he wasn't speaking about the yeast in bread but about the deceptive teaching of the Pharisees and Sadducees.

Not surprising is the disciples' confusion by Jesus' yeast of the Pharisees and Sadducees comment. The surprise is that Jesus tied their confusion to their puny faith. Had their faith been strong, they would have perceived His words' meaning.

Where was the disconnect between their faith and perceiving Jesus' meaning? They had all witnessed two great miracles when Jesus miraculously provided food for thousands of people. Those events were supposed to build faith in the people who witnessed them. The disciples had been integrally involved in both those epic events. Their faith should have been strong enough that they would never again worry about having bread when Jesus was with them. Their mistake was in not being aware that the same Jesus who fed more than nine thousand people was certainly willing to feed His twelve closest friends.

Because they misinterpreted Jesus' meaning about the leaven of the Pharisees and Sadducees, they were missing the warning He was giving them. The Pharisees and Sadducees were hypocrites. They pretended outwardly to be something different from who they were in their hearts. Hypocrisy has no place in the life of a Jesus follower. He was warning them to resist any urge they would ever have to be hypocrites. That's a common and timeless temptation, and we haven't been exempted from it.

> **The lesson of the day was that correct perception of God's Word requires brilliant faith.**

The twelve had either forgotten Jesus' power to miraculously feed people or become unaware that He still carried the same miracle-working power that He used in the mass feeding miracles. Or maybe it was both. Regardless, they had lost their familiarity and their awareness. Remembering what we know about God is important. Since they didn't re-

58

member, the disciples' brilliant faith had become puny; therefore, they didn't perceive what Jesus was saying to them. The lesson of the day was that correct perception of God's Word requires brilliant faith.

Puny Faith Fixes

The Prize	The Punifier	The Scenario	Brilliant Faith Solution
Provision	Worry	Food & Clothing Matthew 6	Know that God will meet your needs as you seek Him.
Protection	Fear	Storm on the Sea Matthew 8	.Remember that Jesus will never leave or forsake us.
Performance	Doubt	Walking on Water Matthew 14	Keep your focus on Jesus, not your circumstances.
Perception	Confusion	Leven of Pharisees Matthew 16	Remember that Jesus may warn His followers, but He won't condemn us.

Personal Application

- Which is usually the most challenging to your faith:

    Worrying about provision?

    Fearing for protection?

    Doubting you can perform what God has called you to do?

    Misunderstanding/misapplying God's Word because of losing sight of who He is and what He's done?

- Which facet of brilliant faith do you need to strengthen to overcome that challenge?

─10─

Great

Great faith believes God for the extraordinary.

Two people impressed Jesus with their faith so much that
He said their faith was great. One was a Roman centurion and
the other a Canaanite woman. In this chapter, we look at each
of them to find what it was that made their faith great.

The Roman Centurion

First, the Roman centurion, whose Jesus-encounter we
find in Matthew 8:5-13.

> *Now when Jesus had entered Capernaum, a centurion came to
> Him, pleading with Him, saying, "Lord, my servant is lying at
> home paralyzed, dreadfully tormented." And Jesus said to him,
> "I will come and heal him." The centurion answered and said,
> "Lord, I am not worthy that You should come under my roof. But
> only speak a word, and my servant will be healed. For I also am
> a man under authority, having soldiers under me. And I say to
> this one, 'Go,' and he goes; and to another, 'Come,' and he comes;
> and to my servant, 'Do this,' and he does it." When Jesus heard
> it, He marveled, and said to those who followed, "Assuredly, I
> say to you, I have not found such great faith, not even in Israel!
> And I say to you that many will come from east and west, and
> sit down with Abraham, Isaac, and Jacob in the kingdom of
> heaven. But the sons of the kingdom will be cast out into outer*

darkness. There will be weeping and gnashing of teeth." Then Jesus said to the centurion, "Go your way; and as you have believed, so let it be done for you." And his servant was healed that same hour (Matt 8:5-13).

Let's analyze this considering the five facets of brilliant faith.

Familiar. The centurion no doubt had heard of the miracles Jesus had performed in the region of Galilee where he lived. He also had heard of some of His teachings and probably some of the confrontations with hypocritical Jewish leaders. He was familiar with Jesus' willingness to act favorably toward people of lower social standing during that time such as women, lepers, the poor, and tax collectors.

While we may not think of the commander of a battalion of one-hundred Roman soldiers as being on the lower end of the social spectrum, we need to understand that he lived in a Jewish community, that Jews were exclusive and nationalistic in their thinking, and that he wasn't a Jew. He surely understood that. He was aware that Jesus was a Jew who performed all His powerful, compassionate miracles for Jews. He must have also known that Jesus responded favorably to faith. Maybe he thought Jesus might value his faith over his social standing. He knew Jesus operated with unlimited authority and that His authority transcended space and distance.

Aware. The centurion had heard that Jesus was near his residence, and he was aware that Jesus was soon to be present and accessible to him.

Invoke. The Roman soldier engaged Jesus, telling Him about his paralyzed young servant, and asked Jesus to heal him.

Trust. The centurion not only trusted that Jesus could heal his servant, but also that He could heal him without going to his house, by just speaking the commanding word from where He was.

Heed. The first response the centurion had to Jesus was an attempt to redirect Him. We wouldn't normally think that redirecting God would be an appropriate response to Him, but the centurion did it with humility and with a sense of awe of Jesus' power, divinity, and authority. His second response to Jesus was to go home when Jesus told him that his servant was healed, trusting that Jesus had accomplished what He said He had.

The centurion demonstrated brilliant faith. His faith was pumping on all cylinders. What made his brilliant faith great was that he believed Jesus to go beyond His normal scope of working miracles.

The Gentile Woman

Then Jesus left Galilee and went north to the region of Tyre and Sidon. A Gentile woman who lived there came to Him, pleading, "Have mercy on me, O Lord, Son of David! For my daughter is possessed by a demon that torments her severely." But Jesus gave her no reply, not even a word. Then his disciples urged him to send her away. "Tell her to go away," they said. "She is bothering us with all her begging." Then Jesus said to the woman, "I was sent only to help God's lost sheep—the people of Israel." But she came and worshiped Him, pleading again, "Lord, help me!" Jesus responded, "It isn't right to take food from the children and throw it to the dogs." She replied, "That's true, Lord, but even dogs are allowed to eat the scraps that fall beneath their master's table." "Dear woman," Jesus said to her, "your faith is great. Your request is granted." And her daughter was instantly healed (Matt. 15:21-28 NLT).

Now let's look at the Gentile woman's faith through the five facets.

Familiar. The woman had obviously heard of Jesus' power to deliver the demon-possessed and set them free.

Aware. News must've travelled fast when the Deliverer came to town, so the woman became aware that He was near.

Invoke. The Gentile woman met some resistance when she invoked Jesus. It didn't get any easier for her when she sought an audience with the disciples. Her invoking included persistence, which was a defining characteristic of her great faith. Her conversation with Jesus could be characterized as a debate in which she answered His every objection with an "I'm not leaving until You say yes" attitude. What we can learn from her is that invoke can require multiple efforts.

Trust. After demonstrating her unwavering patience, she heard Jesus tell her that her request was granted. Then she went away satisfied. Her going away proved that she trusted Jesus' promise, although I suppose we could say her greatest display of trust was in her persistence, since she persisted to obtain what she trusted, Jesus' promise to free her daughter from a tormenting devil.

Heed. She heeded Jesus' assertion that she, as a Gentile, didn't have access to the Jews' table on which the miracles of Christ were served, even though she pressed Him to allow her to receive what was left over from their table.

Personal Application

- What do you need God to do in your life that would be not only miraculous, but out of the ordinary, even for God's miracles?

- The centurion's great faith removed space and distance, and the woman's great faith persisted through all racial, ethnic, and social barriers. What does your brilliant faith need to do to become great?

−11−

Saving

The most important faith saves us from eternal destruction and into eternal life with God.

Spending eternity with God, rather than apart from Him, is the most important need we have. Our earthly lives are filled with significance, but if we're choosing between this life and the next one, it's an easy decision. It's simple math: Infinity > 120 years (the longest life anyone is likely to live here). Yet in this life we hold the seed for eternity in what faith we choose. Choosing brilliant faith is choosing saving faith. Through the five facets of brilliant faith, we can see how that's true. Let's view my own experience, that I conveyed in Chapter 7 Comes and Grows, to see how brilliant faith was, and is, my saving faith.

> In this life we hold the seed for eternity in what faith we choose.

Familiar. I became familiar with the power of the name of Jesus, learned that He had power over the enemy of my soul, and realized that He cared for me enough to rescue me.

Aware. I had experienced the reality of God showing up for me, and I was aware the He invited me to become His child.

Invoke. I asked God to save me.

Trust. After the Holy Spirit convicted me of my sins and I confessed my sins, I trusted that God had forgiven me and accepted me.

Heed. The Holy Spirit prompted me to surrender my life to Jesus and repent from my sinful heart and accept God's forgiveness. I responded to His prompting with obedience.

Saving Faith in Three Thousand People

Now let's see the saving faith of some other people—three thousand of them. In Acts 2, Jesus has been raised from the grave, and He's appeared three separate times to His followers. The last time He was with them, He told them to remain in Jerusalem, to wait there for the heavenly Father to give them the Holy Spirit. We now find them there waiting in obedience to Jesus' instructions.

On the day of Pentecost all the believers were meeting together in one place. Suddenly, there was a sound from heaven like the roaring of a mighty windstorm, and it filled the house where they were sitting. Then, what looked like flames or tongues of fire appeared and settled on each of them. And everyone present was filled with the Holy Spirit and began speaking in other languages, as the Holy Spirit gave them this ability.

At that time there were devout Jews from every nation living in Jerusalem. When they heard the loud noise, everyone came running, and they were bewildered to hear their own languages being spoken by the believers. They were completely amazed. "How can this be?" they exclaimed. "These people are all from Galilee, and yet we hear them speaking in our own native languages! Here we are—Parthians, Medes, Elamites, people from

Mesopotamia, Judea, Cappadocia, Pontus, the province of Asia, Phrygia, Pamphylia, Egypt, and the areas of Libya around Cyrene, visitors from Rome (both Jews and converts to Judaism), Cretans, and Arabs. And we all hear these people speaking in our own languages about the wonderful things God has done!" They stood there amazed and perplexed. "What can this mean?" they asked each other. But others in the crowd ridiculed them, saying, "They're just drunk, that's all!"

Then Peter stepped forward with the eleven other apostles and shouted to the crowd, "Listen carefully, all of you, fellow Jews and residents of Jerusalem! Make no mistake about this. These people are not drunk, as some of you are assuming. Nine o'clock in the morning is much too early for that. No, what you see was predicted long ago by the prophet Joel: 'In the last days,' God says, 'I will pour out my Spirit upon all people. Your sons and daughters will prophesy. Your young men will see visions, and your old men will dream dreams. In those days I will pour out my Spirit even on my servants—men and women alike—and they will prophesy. And I will cause wonders in the heavens above and signs on the earth below—blood and fire and clouds of smoke. The sun will become dark, and the moon will turn blood red before that great and glorious day of the Lord arrives. But everyone who calls on the name of the Lord will be saved.'

People of Israel, listen! God publicly endorsed Jesus the Nazarene by doing powerful miracles, wonders, and signs through him, as you well know. But God knew what would happen, and his prearranged plan was carried out when Jesus was betrayed. With the help of lawless Gentiles, you nailed him to a cross and killed him. But God released him from the horrors of death and raised him back to life, for death could not keep him in its grip. King David said this about him: 'I see that the Lord is always with me. I will not be shaken, for he is right beside me. No wonder my heart is glad, and my tongue shouts his praises! My body rests in hope. For you will not leave my soul among the dead or allow your Holy One to rot in the grave. You have shown me the way of life, and you will fill me with the joy of your presence. Dear brothers, think about this! You can be sure that the patriarch David wasn't referring to himself, for he died and was buried, and his tomb is still here among us. But he was a prophet, and he knew God had promised with an oath that one of David's own descendants would sit on his throne. David was looking into the future and speaking of the Messiah's resurrection. He was saying that God would not leave him among the dead or allow his body to rot in the grave. God raised Jesus from the dead, and we are all witnesses of this. Now he is exalted to the place of highest honor in heaven, at God's right hand. And the Father, as he had promised, gave him the Holy Spirit to pour out upon us, just as you see and hear today. For David himself never ascended into heaven, yet he said, 'The Lord said to my Lord, "Sit in the place of honor at my right hand until I humble your enemies, making them a footstool under your feet. So let everyone in Israel know for certain that God has made this Jesus, whom you crucified, to be both Lord and Messiah!" Peter's words pierced their hearts, and they said to him and to the other apostles, "Brothers, what should we do?"

Peter replied, "Each of you must repent of your sins, turn to God, and be baptized in the name of Jesus Christ to show that you have received forgiveness for your sins. Then you will receive the gift of the Holy Spirit. This promise is to you, and to your children, and even to the Gentiles—all who have been called by the Lord our God." Then Peter continued preaching for a long time, strongly urging all his listeners, "Save yourselves from this crooked generation!" Those who believed what Peter said were baptized and added to the church that day—about 3,000 in all (Acts 2:1-41 NLT).

Let's see their saving faith through the five facets.

Familiar. Whether these Jews knew the prophesies of Joel and of David, or if they were hearing them for the first time, they now knew that God had planned and foretold that He would pour His Spirit out upon His people, that they would prophesy and God would do miraculous things, and that those who called on the Lord would be saved. They also now knew Jesus Christ, whom David foretold as being the everlasting King, had risen from the tomb.

Aware. Those Jewish people who spoke languages other than Hebrew became aware that God was present and active when they understood the Galilean believers as they spoke of God's miraculous works in a language the Holy Spirit gave them as He enabled and prompted them to speak. They also knew that God was making them aware of who Jesus was and what He had done for them.

Invoke. When the people cried out to Peter as to what they should do, they were crying out to God since they recognized that God was using Peter to communicate His truth.

Trust. Once Peter told them that salvation would come as they repented from their sins, turned to God, and were baptized in the name of Jesus Christ to show they'd been forgiven, they trusted that what he said was true.

Heed. The new believers obeyed what Peter told them to do, believing in Jesus and being baptized. Obedience is always the appropriate response to God.

Personal Application

- Write out your experience of gaining saving faith using the five facets of brilliant faith.

- Using the five facets of brilliant faith, write out the experience of a person in the Bible who had saving faith.

–12–

Shield

*Brilliant faith is a shield that protects us from
the flaming arrows of our enemy.*

*Finally, my brethren, be strong in the Lord and in the power of
His might. Put on the whole armor of God, that you may be able
to stand against the wiles of the devil. For we do not wrestle
against flesh and blood, but against principalities, against
powers, against the rulers of the darkness of this age, against
spiritual hosts of wickedness in the heavenly places. Therefore
take up the whole armor of God, that you may be able to with-
stand in the evil day, and having done all, to stand. Above all,
taking the shield of faith with which you will be able to quench
all the fiery darts of the wicked one* (Eph. 6:10-13, 16).

In his letter to the church at Ephesus, Paul addressed doing
battle against our enemy. Our enemy, he wrote, is not a person
or group of people, but an organized kingdom of spiritual be-
ings that are wicked and powerful. Using an analogy of a soldier's armor, he instructed, "Taking the shield of faith with
which you will be able to quench all the fiery darts of the
wicked one" (Eph. 6:16). I love that God stated in His Word
that our faith can extinguish all the enemy's fiery darts, not
just certain ones, but all of them. Whatever the devil throws
at us, brilliant faith can intercept and extinguish.

Close the Door

Of all the pieces of armor Paul could've likened to FAITH, he chose the shield. The Greek word used in that verse for shield refers to a shield in the approximate shape and size of a door. That shield was big enough to protect a soldier's entire body. It's significant that Paul chose that size of shield to represent faith. It means that our faith is sufficient to protect us if we use it. Since brilliant faith is so multifaceted, there isn't a part of our life at any time that it won't protect. It's reliable because it's based on our knowledge of God, and God is completely dependable. Brilliant faith is big enough. With brilliant faith we can close the door completely and not allow the enemy into our lives.

Fiery Darts and the Five-Faceted Shield

Satan has a variety of weapons he uses to attempt to kill, steal, or destroy something in our lives. However, Jesus has armed us with what we need to defend ourselves. To understand how that warfare works, let's look at some of the enemy's fiery darts and see, through the five facets, how brilliant faith extinguishes them. We can see each of the fiery darts in the life of David.

1. Fiery Darts of Intimidation

The gigantic Philistine champion, Goliath, stood taunting the army of Israel day after day, and all of Israel's soldiers were intimidated. Even though King Saul had promised his daughter in marriage and tax exemption for the family of the man who would defeat Goliath, no soldier dared accept Goliath's invitation to fight him one-on-one. But when young David, not even a soldier yet, came to bring some bread to his older brothers who were in the army, he saw Goliath through the eyes of brilliant faith (1 Samuel 15).

Familiar. David was familiar with God's power and commitment to give victory to the nation and army of Israel. He knew of the victorious battles of Jewish history, like Moses, Joshua, and the Amalekites, the conquering of Jericho, and Gideon and the massive Midianite army. If the soldiers had been familiar with the great victories of Israel's past, they had forgotten them, rendering them unfamiliar to them for any practical purpose. David also knew from experience that God had equipped him for magnificent feats of valor, because he had defeated both a lion and a bear during his days of shepherding his father's sheep.

Aware. It was obvious that the Philistine giant disdained the Israelite army, insulting them with his repeated challenge. Everyone heard his insults and felt deep shame as their hearts filled with fear. However, David was aware of something the others weren't. He had a keen sense that the Lord was connected to the Israelite army. They were His army and He, not Abner or Saul, was their leader. Goliath's insults were hurled at God. That was offensive to David, and He was keenly aware that God would help him silence this uncircumcised loudmouth.

Invoke. As David approached Goliath, he warned his hulking foe that he and his army would soon be bird food, and that everyone would know about the God of Israel. As he released those prophesies into the air, I have the sense that they were meant not only to discourage the Philistines but also to encourage the Israelites. They were a call to God to help him accomplish what he was proclaiming.

Trust. David demonstrated that he trusted the Lord with one clear action. He took off running straight to a giant enemy warrior who intended to kill him.

Heed. David's actions in 1 Samuel 17 demonstrate his enthusiastic obedience to God's millennia-long call for His people to trust Him.

2. Fiery Darts of Provocation

King Saul became threatened by David because of his superior military success. That success made David more popular than Saul in the eyes of the Israelites. Saul was jealous and became David's fierce enemy. Saul's jealousy overcame him, and he threw a spear at David in the palace, narrowly missing him. Soon David was on the run with Saul pursuing him for miles. Finally, Saul caught up with him without even knowing it. David was hiding in a cave in the wilderness, and Saul went inside that very cave to relieve himself. As Saul stood with his back to David, and with the men hiding with David urging David to kill Saul, David sneaked up behind Saul and decided to cut off a corner of Saul's robe.

David had the opportunity to kill the one who had sought long and hard to kill him. Nevertheless, he merely cut a piece of the king's robe and eventually bowed before King Saul, confessing he'd done wrong by even cutting the garment of the one whom God had anointed king of His people, Israel.

David's faith extinguished the fiery dart of provocation, avoiding the temptation to become angry and kill his beloved king (1 Samuel 23 and 24).

Familiar. David knew God highly valued those He had anointed for His purposes. He also knew He had anointed Saul to be the king of Israel.

Aware. David's comrades may not have been aware that God's anointing was still upon Saul, but David certainly was. Even though David had been anointed as the next king, he was aware that Saul still stood as the Lord's anointed.

Invoke. Nothing is recorded where David invoked the Lord in the cave that day. Long before David fled into those mountains, he inquired of God whether he should stay where he was or move on to another location, and the Lord's answer indicated that he should move on (1 Samuel 23:9-13).

Trust. David's trust in God was evident by the way he sought His counsel often and followed it each time. It also took some trust in God's protective hand for David to bow himself before Saul in the cave that day.

Heed. When the Lord advised David to go a certain way or do a certain thing, he did as He said.

3. The Fiery Darts of Luring

Bathsheba was bathing in view of King David as he looked out from a palace balcony. David had been victorious against other fiery darts from his enemy, but this one lured him into an adulterous act and the ensuing sin of secretly arranging for the murder of Bathsheba's husband, Uriah (2 Samuel 11 and 12).

Familiar. Through the narrative of David's life in 1 Samuel, 2 Samuel, and 1 Chronicles, and worshipful words of the psalms he wrote, it is obvious that he was deeply familiar with God. He was a man who pursued the very heart of God. All He knew about God would do him no good in this battle because his focus was on taking another man's wife for himself, rather than submitting himself to the God who had given him so many victories.

Consequently, in the hour of need, David's familiarity with God was empty.

Aware. David failed in the aware part of his faith. He missed that God was available to help him overcome the power of the lure. He also got swallowed up by his selfish desire, as if he were oblivious to it.

Invoke. Had David called upon the Lord for help, this would've been a completely different chapter in his story. Unfortunately, he didn't.

Trust. Again, circumstances could've been vastly different had David trusted God's ways over satisfying his sinful pleasure.

Heed. Nope. None.

Interlocking Advantage

My son, Sidney, once spoke in one of our services for people recovering from addiction, and he spoke on spiritual warfare. As he talked about the shield of faith, he invited several people in the audience up with him to help with an illustration.

He had them all gather around him as closely and tightly as they could. They all crouched into a readiness stance, and each held up an imaginary shield as if enemy arrows were being rained down upon them. As they followed his instructions, he demonstrated for the audience that many shields that first century Roman soldiers carried were interlocking. He said ancient Roman soldiers would sometimes gather in groups of four or more and assemble themselves like the volunteers Sidney had brought up.

Their interlocking shields would form a contiguous protective wall in the front, top, and sides of the group, allowing the group to advance toward the enemy even against intense archery attacks.

The point of the illustration was how much more protected we are together than alone. Our faith is powerful, but we still need the help of our fellow soldiers of the faith. We can strengthen one another by encouragement to continue in faith and by using our own faith to pray for each other. We can be an example of faith. At times we may share with each other the faith challenges we face and find support that grows the love and empathy we have for each other. As strong as our brilliant faith is, it's even stronger when we interlock it with the brilliant faith of our brothers and sisters.

> As strong as our brilliant faith is, it's even stronger when we interlock it with the brilliant faith of our brothers and sisters.

Personal Application

- What scripture(s) can you think of that would serve you well against the enemy's attacks?

- What has been the key part of your success in the past against the attacks of the enemy?

─13─

Faithful

Brilliant Faith x Time = Faithful

Being faithful is to fill up our chronological life with brilliant faith. It's brilliant faith not taking a break. If we're going to be faithful followers of Jesus, we must fill up the points along the timeline of our lives with faith in Him. To be faithful we need to be consistently full of faith. In the process, we prove trustworthy and successful.

The Bible talks about God's faithfulness. His faithfulness is different from ours because He doesn't use or need faith. God is faithful in the sense of being consistently trustworthy concerning His Word. He never forgets His promises, instructions, or principles. He never operates in violation of His Word. We can always rely on God keeping His Word. The attributes of God that we are familiar with, we can trust that He will be consistent in without fail. He is supremely faithful, the model of faithfulness.

Trustworthy

"God is not a man, that He should lie, nor a son of man, that He should repent. Has He said, and will He not do? Or has He spoken, and will He not make it good?" (Num. 23:19)

Being faithful means we are trustworthy. It means we've

proven that others can trust us. God is trustworthy; He is faithful. If we'll be trustworthy, it will be because we are consistent in trusting Him.

It may seem backward to say that to be trustworthy we must trust, but it's true. Here's a graphic to illustrate the logic:

God is trustworthy.

We consistently trust God.

As we trust God, others can trust us.

Our consistent trust proves us trustworthy.

We prove our trustworthiness all because we trust God. People consider us faithful because we respond to God's faithfulness. The burden of faithfulness rests on Him. Our job is to always trust Him with it.

The Measure of Success

I like to think of success as having brilliant faith in succession. Time filled with brilliant faith translates to faithfulness, and faithfulness is success with God. When we finally stand before God, we want to hear Him say, "Well done! You've been faithful!" (Matt. 25:23). Our measure of success is successive brilliant faith.

Some situations challenge our faith. On those occasions, it's important to focus on the Lord and deliberately lean into

Him. It's as simple as turning to Him and not to something else. Here are some of those situations:

- When our pain is great.
- When life is mundane and boring.
- When we disappoint ourselves.
- When other people disappoint us.
- When we lose someone we love.
- When we have all we need and lack nothing.
- When we're successful in our goals.
- When we're popular.
- When we're unpopular.
- When our responsibilities are overwhelming.
- When we're tempted to sin.
- When we struggle with anger, resentment, unforgiveness, or covetousness.

Jesus promised to always be with us, and His Spirit is not only with us, but also in us if we have faith in Him. He invites us to throw our cares onto Him—He wants to carry those loads that we can't carry!

Having faith that He is with us and will manage what we can't is our key to success. Being consistent in that faith is the key to successive success.

Daily Bread

Long before David became Israel's famous king, his father

sent him to take some bread to his brothers who were in King Saul's army. Once there, he found that Goliath was humiliating the army daily. Young David ended up fighting and defeating Goliath in an epic moment in biblical, Jewish, and world history. The Philistine giant was challenging Israel to send someone out to fight. Goliath was a one-day battle for David, and David was successful. Imagine having to fight a giant every day.

We don't have to use our imagination very much because that's our reality. We constantly face an ongoing threat of defeat. Fortunately, our God is ever-present and closer to us and more powerful than any enemy or challenge we face. God is never unavailable. We just must remember that we never have to do anything without Him. He is completely trustworthy, so we can be completely faithful.

> **Fortunately, our God is ever-present and closer to us and more powerful than any enemy or challenge we face.**

In Jesus' model prayer, He demonstrated that we should ask our heavenly Father for our daily bread (Luke 11:3). Those words carry more than a literal meaning; they also extend to include other benefits.

We need more than bread every day. Jesus said that people can't live by bread alone, but we also need the words that come from the mouth of God (Luke 4:4). I like to put it this way: Trust God for everything we need with which to serve Him. We can ask and trust God to supply every need we have, whether it's food, money, relationships, transportation, understanding, ability—whatever it is. He wants us to be faithful, and He'll make that possible with every form of support we need.

Jesus' words also establish for us our focus. He wants us to live in today. Preoccupation with yesterday or tomorrow renders us ineffective today. Trusting God for what we need when we need it makes our faithfulness a reality. Regrets of yesterday or worries about tomorrow take us out of the present, the point in time where we can be faithful.

Personal Application

- What is the greatest challenge to your faithfulness?

- What's the most important single adjustment you can make to become more consistent with brilliant faith?

–14–

Beyond

Brilliant faith, even in its completeness,
still cannot contain God.

As powerful and effective as brilliant faith is, God is much greater. It's also true that faith isn't the only thing He wants for us. It's important to recognize, and important enough to designate a short chapter to acknowledge that there is much beyond our faith.

Things God Performs Beyond Our Faith

Fortunately, what God does isn't dependent upon our faith. While it's true that He performs incredible feats in response to our faith, it's also true that He works well beyond the borders of our faith. As impressive as faith is, it doesn't carry the burden of everything God does.

Many things God does require zero faith. Three of His attributes frame many, if not all, of them:

1. His Power

Our faith cannot contain the full power of God. If it could, how limited He would be! Let's give thanks to Him that we don't have to bear that burden.

> God doesn't answer to our faith. In all things, in every way, we and our faith serve Him.

2. His Sovereignty

God doesn't answer to our faith. In all things, in every way, we serve Him and our faith serves Him.

3. His Grace

Paul wrote that we are justified by faith (Rom. 3:28). He certainly didn't mean we are saved without grace. It's God's grace that affords us everything. Brilliant faith merely gives us access to many of His gifts, and some gifts He bestows upon us regardless of faith.

What God Wants for Us
Beyond Our Faith

It's impossible to have brilliant faith without love. If loveless faith is the kind of faith we have, it's worthless. Paul wrote, "If I have a faith that can move mountains, but have not love, I am nothing" (1 Cor. 13:2). God requires something of us that surpasses even faith, and that is love. So, if we're hyper-focused on accomplishing things with our faith, we must remember that if we're leaving love out of the mix, we aren't operating with brilliant faith, and we're missing some of its most important parts and functions.

The brilliant faith I'm describing in this book will always include love because it's based on being familiar with God, and one of the foundational things we know about God is that He loves us and enables us to also love. Still, we can fall into such tunnel vision with our faith that we neglect loving people and even God. So, He reminds us through the New Testament epistles that we must include love with our faith. Paul concluded what is known as the "love chapter" with this: "And now these three remain: faith, hope and love. But the greatest of these is love" (1 Cor. 13:13).

Personal Application

- What are some blessings God has brought into your life that came beyond your faith to believe for them, ask for them, or even know about them?

- What experiences do you remember when you operated in faith with love?

Section 3

TED EESTER

TED EESTER is an acrostic that represents the nine parts of a person's life. It is made up of three larger categories, each with three parts. It's a tool I developed several years ago that I use to manage my spiritual life. I've found it useful, and I hope you'll benefit from it as well.

The first category, TED, is our inner life:
- Thoughts
- Emotions
- Desires

The second category, EES, includes the ways external things enter our inner lives:
- Eyes
- Ears
- Systems

The third category, TER, is our outer life:
- Tongue
- Extremities
- Resources

The nine chapters in this section will offer insight for using your brilliant faith in each part of your life. Faith both affects each part and is affected by each part. This section's primary objective is to help with life application of brilliant faith.

—15—

Thoughts

*A healthy thought life is critical, and brilliant faith
is critical to a healthy thought life.*

As a person thinks in their heart, so are they.
—King Solomon

Our thought life is the most important part of us because
it's where we make decisions.

Decision-making isn't the only thing that happens in our
minds. We also reason, learn, remember, and imagine—all important processes. Our ability to process our thoughts in these
ways depends upon the thought content we are processing.

Putting the wrong kind of fuel in your car not only com-
promises the performance of the engine, but it also can com-
promise the condition of the engine. Likewise, the thought
content we process has an impact on both the performance and
health of our minds. The difference between fuel and thought
is that many more thought content options exist than fuel options. Fuel pumps are clearly labeled, but thought matter doesn't
come tagged with an ID. To be able to discern whether it's good
or bad, we need some way to identify the thought.

God created our minds. He designed them to function very
well, and to do so we need to use them according to the Man-
ufacturer's design. A godly thought environment is a healthy

thought environment, and we can't have a godly thought environment without faith. Faith allows us to perceive what's real and what isn't, what's important and what isn't, and what's good and what isn't. Perception like this is vital for a well-functioning mentality.

Misperceiving means judging something true to be false or vice versa. The difference between misperceiving and perceiving correctly makes the difference in the major directional decisions we all make, the ones related to our education, career, spouse, family, and God. When God spoke through Moses and called the Israelites to make a choice, He was asking them to make a faith choice. He said, "Today I have given you the choice between life and death, between blessings and curses. Now I call on heaven and earth to witness the choice you make. Oh, that you would choose life" (Deut. 30:19). When we think with faith, our healthy minds process constructive thoughts, making choices that produce life.

Thought Content

I love it when God delineates guidelines for us clearly in His Word. Philippians 4:8 is such a passage, where He lists the criteria for godly thought matter: "Fix your thoughts on what is true, and honorable, and right, and pure, and lovely, and admirable. Think about things that are excellent and worthy of praise" (Phil. 4:8 NLT).

Notice that all these criteria are positive. They each have a negative counterpart—false, deplorable, wrong, corrupt, despicable, horrible, second-rate, detestable—but God doesn't want us spending our thoughts on such things. If we fix our thoughts on the positive, we'll recognize the negative more quickly because they'll stick out like a sore thumb. We may need to give some attention to something negative at times, but that's not where God wants us to live. When we recognize an ungodly thought, the Lord wants us to capture it and bring it under His authority. He wants us to judge it unwanted and dispose of it.

Notice, also, that these criteria draw our attention to the things of God, who is not only the source of truth but is also Himself the truth? Who is more deserving of honor? Who is righteous? Who alone is pure? Who is more beautiful? Who inspires more awe? Who excels farther? Who is more worthy of praise? He is indirectly saying: "Fix your eyes on Me and the things of Me." When we do that, our faith is brilliant.

Remember, as King Solomon is quoted above, we are what we think. If we want to be people committed to truth, honorable people, people who do what is right, whose lives aren't contaminated by sinful behaviors, whom people find easy to love and admire, people who excel in our endeavors and are worthy to be commended—if we want to be this kind of people, we should think in these ways. As we think, so shall we be.

The Five Thought Processes

When we think, we are using one or more of five thought processes. Let's deal with them one at a time considering brilliant faith.

1. Reasoning

Reasoning uses the cause-and-effect system to form conclusions. For example, it may establish that a caused b and b caused c. So, a was the reason for b and b was the reason for c. Thus, the term reasoning.

Brilliant faith makes it possible for us to reason that God caused everything to be created, that Jesus caused forgiveness of our sin, that His Word and His Spirit cause Him to be known, that His love causes us to love, and millions more truths that we can fathom only by faith.

> **Brilliant faith is a reasoning model.**

Brilliant faith itself is reasonable. I am familiar with God. Therefore, I am aware of Him in my situation. Therefore, I invoke Him to save me, and I place my trust in Him to do so. Those things cause me to heed Him. Brilliant faith is a reasoning model.

The reasoning that's natural and common in the kingdom of God we don't really get unless we have faith. The Lord prophesied through Isaiah that He would wash away the stains caused by our sins.

"Come now, and let us reason together,'" says the Lord. "'Though your sins are like scarlet, they shall be as white as snow; though they are red like crimson, they shall be as wool'" (Isa. 1:18).

The Lord uses the word *reason* as He invites us to walk through this cause-and-effect with Him, but it takes faith to accept what He's offering. We may understand it on a sheer mental level without faith, but that's not the Lord's goal. His goal is for us to comprehend it so we accept it for ourselves.

Anyone can understand the concept that humanity's sin has caused us to be stained, and God will restore us to purity. Through brilliant faith the Holy Spirit can help us grasp the weight of our sin and the awe-inspiring grace of Jesus removing it for us.

Sitting in my college dorm room after committing my life

to Jesus, only one thing was missing. I didn't understand the seriousness of my sin. As I sat at my desk, the Holy Spirit opened my spiritual eyes and allowed me to see the filthiness of my sin-stained life. Even though I was alone with Him, I was embarrassed and filled with deep regret. All I could do was cry and say "I'm sorry" over and over. God was reasoning with me, showing me that my sin caused great pain, and Jesus' death caused my forgiveness. God and I were reasoning together, just as He had prophesied through Isaiah, but in the most personal, intimate place: in the heart of my thought life. That wasn't the last time the Lord and I reasoned about my sin and His forgiveness. It was the first.

2. Learning

Learning is the process of adding knowledge, wisdom, and skills to ourselves. Proverbs tells us that the way to add knowledge and wisdom is by being familiar with and aware of God to the extent that we have a real and reverent fear of Him (Prov. 1:9-10). Having brilliant faith means we hold God in His rightful place—above all—and are positioned to learn from Him. Brilliant faith makes us teachable.

> **Brilliant faith makes us teachable**

Learning doesn't always happen quickly. It often takes multiple exposures to what God is teaching us. We can see that play out to ridiculous levels as Jesus teaches the disciples about His resurrection:

First Exposure: Despite Jesus stating He would rise again, Peter rebuked Him.

He began to teach them that the Son of Man must suffer many things, and be rejected by the elders and chief priests and scribes, and be killed, and after three days rise again. He spoke this word openly. Then Peter took Him aside and began to rebuke Him (Mark 8 :31-32).

Second Exposure: They were confused, not thinking He meant it.

He taught His disciples and said to them, "The Son of Man is being betrayed into the hands of men, and they will kill Him. And after He is killed, He will rise the third day." But they did not understand this saying, and were afraid to ask Him (Mark 9:31-32).

Third Exposure: Jesus states it most explicitly.

Then He took the twelve aside again and began to tell them the things that would happen to Him: "Behold, we are going up to Jerusalem, and the Son of Man will be betrayed to the chief priests and to the scribes; and they will condemn Him to death and deliver Him to the Gentiles; and they will mock Him, and scourge Him, and spit on Him, and kill Him. And the third day He will rise again" (Mark 10:32-34).

Fourth Exposure: When some women followers report to the disciples that Jesus is not in the tomb and that angels told them He had arisen, they still do not believe.

Now on the first day of the week, very early in the morning, [the women had come with Him from Galilee], and certain other women with them, came to the tomb bringing the spices which they had prepared. But they found the stone rolled away from the tomb. Then they went in and did not find the body of the Lord Jesus. And it happened, as they were greatly perplexed about this, that behold, two men stood by them in shining gar-

ments. Then, as they were afraid and bowed their faces to the earth, they said to them, "Why do you seek the living among the dead? He is not here, but is risen! Remember how He spoke to you when He was still in Galilee, saying, 'The Son of Man must be delivered into the hands of sinful men, and be crucified, and the third day rise again.'" And they remembered His words. Then they returned from the tomb and told all these things to the eleven and to all the rest. It was Mary Magdalene, Joanna, Mary the mother of James, and the other women with them, who told these things to the apostles. And their words seemed to them like idle tales, and they did not believe them. But Peter arose and ran to the tomb; and stooping down, he saw the linen cloths lying by themselves; and he departed, marveling to himself at what had happened (Luke 24:1-12).

Fifth Exposure: When the other disciples report to Thomas that they saw Jesus, he still does not believe. Only after seeing Him later does he believe Jesus rose from the grave.

Then, the same day at evening, being the first day of the week, when the doors were shut where the disciples were assembled, for fear of the Jews, Jesus came and stood in the midst, and said to them, "Peace be with you." When He had said this, He showed them His hands and His side. Then the disciples were glad when they saw the Lord (John 20:19-20).

Now Thomas, called the Twin, one of the twelve, was not with them when Jesus came. The other disciples therefore said to him, "We have seen the Lord" (John 20:24).

So he said to them, "Unless I see in His hands the print of the nails, and put my finger into the print of the nails, and put my hand into His side, I will not believe." And after eight days His disciples were again inside, and Thomas with them. Jesus came, the doors being shut, and stood in the midst, and said, "Peace to you!" Then He said to Thomas, "Reach your finger here, and look at My hands; and reach your hand here and put it into My side. Do not be unbelieving but believing." And Thomas answered and said to Him, "My Lord and my God!" Jesus said to him, "Thomas, because you have seen Me, you have believed. Blessed are those who have not seen and yet have believed" (John 20:24-29).

We shouldn't be too harsh on the disciples. We do have the advantage of viewing their story from the back side of history. They walked through the real story with three major hindrances to their understanding:

• They, along with their fellow Jewish brothers and sisters, expected the Messiah to restore the Israelite kingdom on earth.

• So much of Jesus' teaching was hard to understand since He spoke using parables and other analogical devices that often require further explanation.

• As monumental as Jesus' resurrection was, it wasn't the only bit of new prophetic material He was unloading onto them. They must've felt like we have when we've taken an exam with so much information that it's impossible to know all of it.

Despite an ample supply of excuses for their failure to learn that Jesus would rise from the grave, it remains that their faith was lacking. As ridiculous as they seem as we travel along the chronology of their misgivings, I find similar patterns in my own discipleship. The question for us is: What can we learn from their example? Consider the following points:

• **Look for common denominators in life experiences.**

Truth be told, we aren't any sharper than the disciples were. (Thank God my narrative isn't being recorded for all to read!) One benefit we can gain, though, is to look for multiple exposures to a lesson. It's usually the third exposure when I realize God is teaching me something. First, I'll read something in the Bible. Soon after, I'll hear a song that touches the same point. Then, I'll hear a sermon or comment in a conversation. I've missed lessons many times, but I've also improved in my quickness to recognize them. It's like playing *Name That Tune*. "I can name that tune in . . . three notes." For this, the most important facet of our faith is being aware.

• **Utilize all the ways of learning.** We retain a certain amount of what we read and a certain amount of what we hear. Add them together, and of course, we retain more. Add a visual and it increases again. Add music and it goes up even more. Even if we include all four of those, we still haven't utilized the single most effective way of learning something: *participation*. When we can be kinetically active in learning something, we stand a greater chance of retaining it.

God clarified to the Israelites that they should read, speak, and hear His law repetitively. Jesus also challenged religious leaders in their knowledge of the law. Jesus issued an invitation that makes learning most effective. He said:

> *Come to me, all you who are weary and burdened, and I will give you rest. Take my yoke upon you and learn from me, for I am gentle and humble in heart, and you will find rest for your souls. For my yoke is easy and my burden is light* (Matt. 11:28-30 NIV).

Jesus invites us into the best possible learning situation: sharing in a yoke with Him. What that means for us today is to walk with His Spirit, not just beside us, but inside us. In the closeness of our own thoughts, the Holy Spirit teaches us as we heed Him in our faith.

• **Take time to stop and ask God what it is He wants to teach us** and then listen to Him. It's crazy how much we miss by simply not asking God questions and taking the time to listen to His answers. Invoke Him.

One more thing. Please don't confine the Lord to teaching a certain way. It's altogether possible for Him to do in a moment something that will impact us so profoundly that we'll never forget its lesson. We certainly don't want to miss experiences like those. We just need to keep our faith.

3. Remembering

Remembering is when we reactivate thoughts that were previously active but became inactive. I think of it like a club, the Active Thought Club (ATC). We have a massive number of thoughts that are past members of the ATC. When we bring one of them back into active membership, we "remember" it.

We use this process constantly. Sometimes we remember automatically, and sometimes it takes a lot of concentration and significant effort.

The Lord wants us to remember some things, and some things He wants us to forget. (I think of forgetting as permanently "de-membering" a thought from the ATC. It too is sometimes automatic and sometimes requires great and frequent effort.) Remembering is vital to our faith. We need to re-familiarize ourselves with the character and promises of the Lord. We need to remember to be aware of Him, to invoke Him, to trust Him, and to heed Him. Brilliant faith is vital if we're going to both remember and forget what God wants us to recall and dismiss.

The Israelites were enslaved by the Egyptians for four hundred years until the Lord raised up Moses to deliver them. God wanted them to remember two things about Egypt: their bondage and the miraculous way He delivered them (Ex. 13:3; Deut. 5). The night before their departure, He instituted the Passover meal, which involved specific instructions for preparing the meal by roasting a lamb and baking unleavened bread. The Passover was established as an annual feast celebrating their deliverance from bondage. They were also to paint the lamb's blood on the door frame. All firstborns in Egypt would die that night, but those who obeyed God and placed lamb's blood on the door frame He would pass over, thus the name, Passover.

As that generation of Israelites trekked through the wilderness enroute to the land God promised their ancestors, they faced many challenges: the Egyptian army, the need for food, the need for water, and protection from armies of neighboring people. Instead of remembering their bondage and the miracles God performed to deliver them, however, they remembered the safety and provision they enjoyed during their years of miserable slavery. They didn't use their faith to remember what God wanted them to remember.

Some fifteen hundred years later, Jesus sat with His disciples celebrating the Passover feast. He picked up some unleavened bread and shared it with them, along with some new instructions:

And He took bread, gave thanks and broke it, and gave it to them, saying, "This is My body which is given for you; do this in remembrance of Me." Likewise He also took the cup after supper, saying, "This cup is the new covenant in My blood, which is shed for you" (Luke 22:19-21).

Just as God had instructed the Israelites to remember the misery of their bondage and how powerfully He delivered them from it and into their promised land, Jesus instructs His believers to remember His broken body and poured-out blood that powerfully delivers us from the miserable bondage of our sin and into our promised eternal land. Every time we celebrate the Lord's Supper, we are to remember Jesus. I think it's an innovative idea to remember Him every time we take a meal. We cannot afford to forget what He's done for us, so we should intentionally remember Him very often.

4. Imagining

Imagining is to see with our mind's eye what we cannot see with our physical eye. It is for some people the most expansive process. Imaginations have brought us every invention we enjoy, every building ever built, every road, painting, song, novel—everything that had to be envisioned before it could exist. Imaginations have also brought us what is destructive and immoral.

In my opinion, people who are gifted with very creative minds face a greater challenge in submitting that part of their minds to the Lord than those who aren't as creative. Their strong and wild imaginations present great distractions and temptations, so it requires more self-discipline to submit their imaginations to the Lord. Self-control being a fruit produced in us by the Holy Spirit (Gal. 5:22-23), the key is to be filled with Him, allowing Him strong influence over our inventive minds. Brilliant faith helps us manage and wield our imaginative energies by keeping us focused on God and His desires.

Familiar with Him, we know that He is the head when it comes to using imagination to produce life and beauty. God sparks and fuels our imagination for us.

Ephesians 3:20 says that God is able to do far more than we can imagine Him doing. With God, there's all the room we could ever want, and more, to use our imaginations. No one should ever feel as if God doesn't want us to be creative with our minds. He probably wants us to be more creative than we would imagine (pardon the pun). He just wants us to use our imagination for the same purpose He wants us to use all our resources: His glory. When we glorify Him, we find ourselves most fulfilled because that's what He created us to do; it's our purpose.

Do we sacrifice some areas of imaginative thought when we submit those processes to the Lord? Of course, but as with all sacrifices we make for the Lord, He replaces them with immensely more and better than what we give up for Him. He leads us to fields of imaginative thought that we don't have access to without Him and without faith. Those fields are more beautiful, more inspiring, and more fulfilling for us and for the people who benefit from what we imagine.

I met with a friend who had fallen away from faith. As we sat over coffee, he said, "I'm free now. I can watch pornography and not feel guilty about it."

"But are you free to praise God, as I am?" I questioned.

The look on my friend's face told me he realized he had given up something beautiful for something ugly. That's also the difference between a godly and an ungodly imagination. Ungodliness isn't without pleasure, but that pleasure is always short-term and ends in regret. The pleasure a godly imagination produces never brings guilt and continues into eternity.

5. Deciding

Deciding makes me think of a sculptor. He starts with a block of stone and cuts away the parts he doesn't want, leaving intact the parts he does want until it takes the shape he wants. Decide is a two-part word that means "cut away." It derives from the Latin *de*: "away" and *caedere*, "cut." Deciding is the process of mentally cutting away what we don't want and leaving what we do want. It's the process of elimination.

When the Lord asks us to choose life or death, blessing or curses, He's asking us to cut away death and curses from our life, from our future, from our desires. When Joshua was up in age, he told the Israelites he'd led into the land God promised them to choose whom they would serve. Many idols and false gods were in the land they had settled into, and he was asking them to cut away all other options, except for the Lord God Jehovah.

Brilliant faith tells us enough about God that we know He's always the right choice, and His way is always the right way. Brilliant faith keeps life in such an accurate perspective that decisions are usually obvious. It may take some time of seeking for it to become clear, but if we continue in brilliant faith, we make right decisions.

My brilliant faith led me to decide to follow Christ, but that was only the beginning! Now it leads me to live a life of making decisions to follow Christ.

Personal Application

- Of the five thought processes—reasoning, learning, remembering, imagining, and deciding—which is most conducive for brilliant faith for you, which is most difficult, and why?

- Recall and journal about a time when you know God was giving you direction for your thought life.

−16−

Emotions

Brilliant faith is the tool for managing our emotions.

Move Out

The word *emote* means "move out" (*e*: out; *mote*: move). Our emotions are triggered movements occurring within our neurological system, each movement carrying with it a unique sensation or feeling. They originate in the mind, manifest in the brain, and then travel into and through other parts of the body. They often move us to act or react in some way. Further, our emotional actions can trigger emotions in other people that result in their own actions. So, emotions begin from within the heart of our minds and can move all the way out to and through other people and communications technology, to the farthest distances in the world. A lot is moving out when it comes to emotions.

I once preached a sermon series on loving God with all our heart, soul, mind, and strength. The part on loving Him with all our heart was the most fun I've ever had in my preaching ministry. The Hebrew meaning for the word translated *heart* includes "the seat of emotions." I explained the Hebrew meaning of that word and the meaning of the word emote. Then I ran to the back of the sanctuary and out the main doors where a cool red electric scooter (like a small motorcycle) awaited me.

I jumped on and drove it back into the room. I zoomed up and down all the aisles and back and forth across the front and back of the room. The people in the congregation were entertained by it, but not as much as I was.

Eventually, I parked it right in front of the stage. Then I explained that emotions are like scooters. They present themselves to us and invite to us to hop on and take a ride. Each one is a unique situation and has its own amount of horsepower. Each has a seat, handlebars, a throttle, and a brake.

With each one, we have a decision or a series of decisions to make, and it can be of the utmost importance that we make the decisions logically rather than emotionally, that we control our emotions instead of the other way around.

Move Us

Emotions are neutral, neither good nor bad. The system of emotions is just as much a part of us as our circulatory and skeletal systems are. Still, like with our thought life, we must be in control of our emotional life; otherwise, our feelings will rule us and that isn't their purpose. Their purpose is to motivate us to act in response to whatever stimulates them, but we need to manage that process. The problem is they don't have any built-in controls. If they will serve their purpose with positive results, it will be because we're controlling them by the influence of the Holy Spirit, and we'll accept His influence only by faith.

Four Questions

When managing our emotions, we need to answer four questions. They have to do with four concepts: existence, direction, intensity, and duration.

- **Question #1 (Existence):** Should I give any attention to this emotion?

My son, Jacob, has a strong heart, but his heart is also incredibly soft. Our whole family loves that about him. I remember when Jake was about eight or nine years old. He was at a stage of transition from little boy to big boy. I noticed that he would still cry even when he had minor pain. I watched him carefully a few times to be sure I was judging it correctly and decided that I was. Then I had a single conversation with Jacob.

"Jake, I feel as though you're crying sometimes when you don't really need to. Try not to cry when something hurts you only a little bit. You can handle some pain without tears. If the pain becomes too great to hold it back, then go ahead and cry. It's fine to cry, but you don't want to cry at minor things."

Jacob listened to what I said to him and nodded. From that point on, I saw him gain control over his tears. I was proud of him and impressed with his ability to exercise such control just by making the decision on that one day to do so. Each time he had a pain, he made a mental decision whether he should acknowledge it with sadness or not. Sometimes he cried; sometimes he didn't. He learned to manage the emotion that came from his pain.

The very first step in managing any emotion is deciding whether you're going to acknowledge it at all, whether you will allow it to exist. When I preached my scooter sermon, I pointed out that sometimes you just need to declare, "I'm not getting on that scooter!"

Determining the source, the stimulus, of the emotion is helpful in deciding whether it should exist. Being happy about someone's demise or saddened by a person's success are examples of emotions we should let die.

One more thing about existence before we go further. Be careful to not merely ignore a stimulus that needs to be dealt with. A tragic takeaway from this would be that you find yourself in denial about a stimulus and emotion that need to be dealt with. Be sure to seek God's counsel, and the counsel of a wise and qualified person or people to make sure you aren't harboring something unresolved.

- **Question #2 (Direction):** Where does my emotional energy need to be directed?

Misdirecting an emotion, which can easily happen if we aren't controlling it, is as common as it is dangerous. Even though my dad was a good husband and dad in most every other way, he had a temper problem that led to some relational problems that proved exceedingly difficult to overcome. He was ambitious and took some heavy risks as he grew our farm operation. When the financial pressures came, which were often and could be lengthy, he often relieved his stress through anger directed toward his family.

A better question is, "Where does God want me to direct this emotion?" Being familiar and aware of God during emotional floods helps us remember to ask for (invoke) His counsel and direction. Then, of course, it's just a matter of trusting and heeding His response.

- **Question #3 (Intensity):** How intense does my emotional energy need to be?

Jesus was appalled by what was taking place in the temple. His anger burned at the sight of merchants who had taken over the temple, a place intended for worship and prayer. He allowed His anger to energize Him with great intensity, turning over the merchants' tables, chairs, and money then running them out of the temple with a whip He had fashioned right there and for that purpose.

A religious mob came to Gethsemane to apprehend Jesus, which led to His trial, beatings, and crucifixion. In zealous defense of his beloved leader, Peter cut off the ear of one of the men who happened to be the servant of the high priest. Jesus instructed him to put his sword away and placed the man's ear back in its place and healed it. He knew the time had come for His suffering on a cross.

God knows when we need more and when we need less emotional intensity, and He will lead us by His Spirit in each situation. This is yet another area where being familiar and aware of Him, invoking Him for direction, and trusting and heeding His leading will make the difference between being in step with Him and missing the mark with our intensity level.

- **Question #4 (Duration):** How long should I exert my emotional energy?

My parents' deaths hit me hard. I mourned their loss heavily for seventeen months. Some people may read that and say, "That's not all that long to grieve someone you love." To others it may seem like a long time to grieve. I've learned that grieving never really ends, if we remember our lost loved one. I had reached the place where my grieving was keeping me focused on the past. I felt as if the Holy Spirit was beginning to challenge me to look forward more, but I was having trouble cooperating.

My parents left us in April 2015. In December 2016, our son Nate and his wife, Haley, came home from the mission field in Mexico for Christmas. They gave my wife, Sharlene, and me a little souvenir. When we opened it, we saw the words Grandma and Grandpa. Pleasantly surprised, Sharlene and I looked at each other trying to process this life-changing announcement. Suddenly, I blurted out, "This changes everything!"

Titus is our first grandchild and not yet three years old, and boy has he changed everything in the Tew Crew! But my response at the announcement that Nate and Haley were expecting a baby was deeply personal. In that moment, something shifted in me. I made an inward turn from a past-focused mentality to a forward-focused one.

Daily weeping in the early morning hours subsided. I still held a tender spot in my heart for my parents, but my sadness went from deep to shallow. It was time for that deep sadness to end, and the Holy Spirit led me out of it. Thankfully, He gave me a new buddy named Titus who changed my life.

S-A-F-E

All this analysis of emotions, some of which is admittedly subjective, may seem irrelative and boring; the point is that the system of human emotions is incredibly complex. It is a testimony of the supremely advanced and sophisticated skill God uses in crafting people. I don't have the capacity to understand, let alone write about, emotions with any thoroughness. So, I'll simplify the subject into more practical terms.

My printer requires just four cartridges: red, blue, yellow, and black. If they all have ink, it can print any color there is. While there are countless emotions, you will be SAFE if you manage well these four: sadness, anger, fear, and elation. I see all emotions as some combination of these four.

Sadness

James 4 contains specific areas in which the readers' lives should be transformed. He was addressing their ungodly lifestyle, their conformity to the world, and instructing them in very certain terms how they were to correct it. In verse nine he tackled their emotions. They had been laughing joyfully at their pride, violence, and greed, which are sins that should bring believers to sorrow. Their circumstances called for them to discontinue those emotions and replace them with mourning and gloom, and that's exactly what James admonished them to do. He was calling for them to be transformed in their emotions.

As a college junior I had reached the end of myself during the early morning hours of a Monday and was miraculously rescued by the power of Jesus. After such an amazing, eye-opening experience, I made up my mind that I would surrender my life to Him, so I did. I was invited to a midnight prayer meeting in some guys' room in our dormitory. I went up there, knelt, and gave my life—everything I was and would be—to Christ. Afterwards, my roommate, Ted, and I went back down to our room. Ted had decided at the last minute that he would go too, and he renewed his commitment to the Lord in that same prayer meeting.

Once in our room, Ted and I told each other about the commitments we had made. Then after a couple of minutes of blank silence, Ted stood up and said, "We don't know what to do now. I'm going back up there and get some Scriptures from those guys." He opened the door and I stopped him.

"Ted, you gotta tell them I'm scared. I asked God to save me up there, but I don't think He did. I know I've done a lot of terrible things to Him. I've blasphemed Him before, and I'm afraid He's rejected me."

"I'll tell 'em." He walked out and closed the door. Then I heard him open and walk out the suite door, and it closed behind him. I was sitting at my desk in silence, worried and feeling very much alone.

Suddenly, rushing into my mind like a catastrophic flood came all the trash and filth of my life. I was seeing what seemed like everything I had ever thought or done against God, whether in rebellion or apathy. As I saw it all, it devastated me. I was astounded at my guilt. I couldn't hold back my emotions; I exploded into tears and wept uncontrollably.

"I'm sorry! I'm sorry!" was all I could say, and I repeated it over and over between sobs.

Second Corinthians 7:10 (NLT) says, "The kind of sorrow God wants us to experience leads us away from sin and results in salvation. There's no regret for that kind of sorrow." That's the kind of sorrow I had that night. The Holy Spirit was revealing to me my unbearable guilt before God. I was ashamed of it and terribly sorry for the immense pain I imagined I must have inflicted in the heart of the God who had been nothing but good to me.

The Holy Spirit wasn't only showing me my sin in its true ugliness, allowing me to abhor it in the way God does, but he also was leading me to turn away from it and turn to God. I wanted freedom from the guilt and shame, freedom from the pain of its consequences, and freedom from its presence in my future. I was desperate for the freedom to be with God, with nothing being between us. I wanted all this out of the way! And suddenly . . . it was. I knew I was forgiven and God had accepted me.

By the time I had processed all this, I heard Ted reenter the suite and open the door to our room.

He looked at me and saw my swollen red eyes.

"I'm okay. God saved me."

Ted had indeed gotten some Scriptures, and we began our journey. God had done, and continued doing, a major transformation in both of us. Through the ensuing weeks of learning and growing, we enjoyed the experiences of perpetual change God made in us. Among the most noticeable to me were the changes in what naturally sparked various emotions in me. For example, things that had brought laughter before, such as stories of what friends had done when they were drunk, now touched a sad spot in my heart. It's satisfying to have our sorrows match up more closely with the sorrows of the Lord.

Anger

Be angry, and do not sin': do not let the sun go down on your wrath, nor give place to the devil (Eph. 4:26-27).

Be angry, but do not sin in your anger. Don't let it linger longer than necessary for accomplishing its purpose, and don't let it linger in your heart.

Here are five biblical principles regarding anger:

- **Principle #1: Anger belongs to God.**

All emotions belong to God, but anger is one that proves particularly challenging to humans. It's the dynamite of emotions. It blows up whatever it hits. Do a search of the words anger and angry in the Bible, and you'll see that more than 95 percent of the time they have to do with God's anger. In His perfection, He manages anger with ideal placement, timing, and intensity. He is slow to anger allows people multiple opportunities to turn to Him before He executes His wrath.

Anger is best when it's in God's hands, so we should make sure we submit ours to Him and let Him direct us as we manage it.

- **Principle #2: Anger is an emotion we should most often not accept.**

A critical issue for U.S. presidential candidates is their philosophy of using military action in foreign relations. A candidate too quick to pull the trigger to go to war will hopefully never be elected. Who wants a volatile hothead as Commander-in-Chief?

Neither do we want to use anger too quickly. Being the explosive emotion that it is, it will do damage. If the situation doesn't call for something to be damaged, we don't need to accept the invitation to become angry. If its draw is overwhelming, chopping wood, hitting the heavy bag, or vigorously cleaning house are good outlets.

But now you are to put off all these things: anger, wrath, malice, blasphemy, filthy language out of your mouth (Col. 3:8).

- **Principle #3: We should be slow to become angry.**

A foolish person allows just any old thing to set them off. We need to be very resilient to anger, meaning a whole lot of offenses must just roll of our backs like water off a duck. If we're strong in our faith, what should make us angry will be something that angers God too.

Anger isn't something that should linger on for very long. It's too intense, and our minds and bodies aren't made to endure such stress. We need to take the time necessary to process how to respond to the anger stimulus without prolonging it. If we can't resolve it quickly, we need to find a way to let it go.

Sometimes it can be just that simple. With God's help, we can just let go of whatever has angered us, and the anger departs along with it.

He who is slow to anger is better than the mighty, and he who rules his spirit than he who takes a city (Prov. 16:32).

- **Principle #4: We should give adequate thought and prayer to how we're going to resolve anger, then resolve it quickly.**

We're instructed not let the sun go down on our anger. I think God means that in two senses. First, resolve an anger-related issue quickly. Second, resolve it completely; don't abandon the resolution process until it's been fully handled. Leaving a small part of an offense unresolved can be like leaving a little splinter in your foot. It'll get worse before long, and it'll be more difficult to resolve later. If someone has mistreated us, causing us pain and subsequent anger, the wise move is to talk with them about every little part of the offense and reach resolution (by either forgiveness or restitution) before finishing with it. If the issue is more complicated, don't let the figurative sun go down before processing it. In other words, don't move on with life and not deal with it. If we do that, it can fester and cause problems for us in our own hearts and in interpersonal relationships, and we may not even remember where those problems are coming from when they rear their ugly heads long after their season should've ended.

Be angry and do not sin. Meditate within your heart on your bed and be still (Ps. 4:4).

Be angry and do not sin. Do not let the sun go down on your wrath (Eph. 4:26).

- **Principle #5: We have a responsibility not to provoke others to anger.**

Parents have a specific responsibility not to sow seeds of anger in the hearts of their children. The parent-child relationship is critical, vulnerable, and in the crosshairs of our enemy's weapons. The best guard we parents have in protecting our kids' hearts is assuring that they understand that we love them, especially when we discipline them.

We have this same responsibility to all the people who aren't our kids. Jesus taught that even worshiping God can wait for us to resolve a heart issue we may have caused for someone. He made a connection between someone having hatred in their heart and the worshiper who shares some responsibility in that person's heart condition. We are responsible, not only for our own hearts, but also how we affect the hearts of the people in our lives.

Fathers, do not provoke your children to anger by the way you treat them (Eph. 6:4 NLT).

Fear

The Bible relates fear, whether the presence or the absence of fear, in some way to God. If fear is going to be used in our lives the way God wants it to be, we need to model our use of that emotion after the biblical standard. So, we want to fear only what God says to fear, and we want not to fear what He says to not fear. God wants us to fear Him alone, to recognize Him as supreme and able to protect us from whomever or whatever we might otherwise fear.

The fear of God is distinct from every other fear. The fear of the Lord always results in surrender to Him and being His servant. To every person who is His servant, He becomes their friend. So, the fear of the Lord isn't fearful at all. Just the opposite. Rather, a freedom and a peace accompany those who fear God. The one who fears the Lord also possesses a reverence of God that doesn't let anything or anyone else take His rightful place in their life, their heart's throne.

Elation

When we've been transformed by God, some circumstances affect us completely differently from how they did when we conformed to the image of the unbelieving world. The classic example of this is what I call the "James 1234 Principle." It comes from James 1:2, 3, 4, which says that when we realize God is growing our faith and patience through our various trials, our joy also grows. Through James, the Lord is teaching us a new system of values. What we had seen as a liability we now count as an asset. Difficult trials are in the liability column when we lack faith. We're unfamiliar with God as our loving trainer, unaware of His presence in our situation; therefore, we don't reach out to Him, we don't trust Him because we lack basis (familiarity) for trusting Him, and we don't heed Him because we're out of touch with Him.

As I'm writing this paragraph, I'm going through the most difficult trial of my life. I had a major stroke four months ago. My left shoulder, hand, and fingers are still not working. My faith has been hotly tested, and I've wavered several times in believing that God will answer my prayer that He'll heal me.

Despite that, this morning I awoke, spent time alone with God, took Communion, prayed, and studied Scripture. I eventually became elated as I remembered how much God loves me and has demonstrated His love for me over and over. I had such a powerful sense of His presence and involvement that I raised my right hand high and my left as high as I could, dancing and praising God. The Lord has helped me move this trial from the liability column (in my mind) to the asset column. I see that this trial is stretching my faith, and I'm confident I'll come through the fiery trial with greater patience, stronger faith, and more love for God. As I see the value of the trial through a lens of brilliant faith, I value it and am elated by it. That's the James 1234 Principle at work in my life.

Personal Application

- With which of the S-A-F-E emotions do you most need God's help controlling?

- Spend some time in prayer talking with God about your emotional life. Ask Him to show you where you need to make changes. Then ask Him to lead you by His Spirit in making those changes. Be prepared to identify His involvement and to respond appropriately to Him.

~17~

Desires

*Since our desires serve to direct us,
our brilliant faith should direct our desires.*

A Universal Target: Our Desires

Its luscious fruit would be delicious. Had she ever seen anything more beautiful? And talk about healthy! This fruit boosted brain power to divine levels! She was convinced. So, she took the fruit and ate it. (See Genesis 3:6.)

How did Eve come to see the tree in that light? God had made it clear to her and her husband that the tree was the only off-limits plant in the garden because it would bring death.

The lioness knows instinctively exactly where to sink her fangs into the gazelle. She clamps her powerful jaws down on its neck. Once the cat is on the neck, her prey dies by suffocation, blood loss, or both. The neck—that's the target.

Our adversary, the one who goes around like a roaring lion seeking whom he may devour (1 Peter 5:8), knows where to focus his attack: our desires. He targeted Eve's desires and his instincts were correct: if he could get her to desire the tree, she would end up eating the fruit of disobedience and destruction. Our desires are the strategic target; if the devourer can stimulate them, they'll do the rest of his work.

Our desires are a powerful force within us. With rare exception, we choose to do what our strong desires dictate. Those who stand to benefit from our choosing their fruit place a premium value on our desires. So, they go to great lengths to turn our desires in their direction.

Advertisers spend around two hundred billion dollars a year in the U.S.—more than any U.S. state's entire annual budget—hoping their investments will stimulate consumers' desires for whatever they're selling. Businesses aren't the only ones trying to influence people's desires. We all want to be wanted and to be chosen. I certainly do.

When I asked Sharlene to go out on our first date, I hoped she would want to go. I've wanted prospective employers to choose me. I like to be chosen in pickup basketball games and to receive invitations to gatherings I enjoy. So, I put my best foot forward, in hopes of being likeable, of being desirable in each of those scenarios. I don't want to manipulate anyone, but I do invest in being wanted. I spend time and energy making myself desirable, as everyone does.

Entities want so badly to win people's desires that they're willing to compete for them. The advertiser who turns consumers' attention to their product does so by being shrewder, more creative, or harder working than their competitors. Employers sometimes have hundreds of applicants for a single position, and the winner of the job is the person who captured the employer's desire. Desires is an extremely competitive market. Win those and you win people.

In no market is the competition fiercer than the one in which we

> In no market is the competition fiercer than the one in which we make faith decisions about Jesus.

118

make faith decisions about Jesus. Our enemy goes straight for our desires, and he'll do whatever God will allow in attempt to turn our desires his way and away from Jesus. God wants our desires to be for Him, however, and He competes for them too.

Opposing Strategies: Truth vs. Deception

Before the lioness ever attacks, she gets the gazelle separated from the herd. That's her strategy. Gazelles that remain in the thick of the herd are safe. The lioness would be at a disadvantage there.

Our safety lies in having faith in God's Word. The enemy's first step in leading Eve into sin was to separate her from God's Word.

"Has God said . . .?"

"Yes."

"That's not true."

That's the structure of Satan's conversational strategy. He's used it throughout human history, and he still follows it today because it's worked for him. He works extremely hard to separate us from God's Word.

The enemy's next step, once the seed of doubting God's Word is planted, is to stimulate in us a desire for something destructive. He wants us to desire something we would deem detestable if our faith in God's Word were strong. The tree was detestable through the lens of truth, and the truth was that it would bring death. By pulling away from the truth lens and looking instead through the lens of deception, Eve saw beautiful, desirable fruit. If Satan can get us to pull away from God's Word, abandoning the basis of our faith, he can confuse us enough to stimulate within us a desire for evil.

Once we have a desire for something ungodly, Satan is no longer our opponent. At that point, our opponent is our own desire. How formidable that opponent is! James 1:14-15 says, "Each one is tempted when, by his own evil desire, he is dragged away and enticed. Then, after desire has conceived, it gives birth to sin; and sin, when it is full-grown, gives birth to death." Strong desires are so powerful within us that once conceived, they give birth.

> **Once we have a desire for something ungodly, Satan is no longer our opponent. At that point, our opponent is our own desire.**

I watched my wife give birth to all six of our children. At no point in her times of labor could I have said, "Wait a minute, honey. Don't deliver the baby yet. Just hold off for a few minutes."

Nor can we keep a child from growing up. When our daughter, Kristin, was five years old, I realized she was growing up faster than I wanted. I missed the way she had mispronounced her brother's name and was now pronouncing it correctly. Her interests were changing, and she was becoming more independent. I wasn't ready for her to be a big girl. The changes were just happening too fast for me. Kristin loved Barbie dolls, so I offered her one thousand Barbies if she would stop growing up for a little while. She wouldn't take the deal. She and I both knew it wasn't possible anyway.

Ungodly desires conceived, birthed, and allowed to grow are monsters. They're next to impossible to control. Satan knows that and that's why he works to stimulate an evil desire in us. That's why he employs his triple-D strategy: Deception

> Desire > Death. Deception leads to an evil desire, which leads to death if unchecked.

God's strategy is to tell us the truth and help us believe it. Unlike the deceiver, He even shares His strategy with us. A thread that runs all the way through the Bible is the promise that our obedience to God's Word will protect us. A strong section of that thread is Psalm 119. It's the longest chapter in the Bible (176 verses) and reminds us of the advantages of heeding God's Word. Verse 11 says, "Your Word I have hidden in my heart that I might not sin against You." He hid God's Word in his heart, so the enemy couldn't separate him from it.

Three Keys to Having Godly Desires
Key #1 – Yield Your Will

Even though Adam and Eve were created without sin, they were still vulnerable. All of humankind has needed God's help from the very beginning. Paul wrote of our "desires dilemma" in Romans 7. In the last two verses of that chapter, he gives the solution—Jesus Christ.

Jesus came and provided the help we need most. In addition to freeing us from the penalty of sin, He taught us how we should live. He said we should pray for the Father's will to be done on earth just as it is in heaven. When Jesus came to the eve of His brutal death, He demonstrated how to deal with our desires.

He went to the garden of Gethsemane in the evening to pray. Distraught with the knowledge of the agony He would endure a few hours later, He asked the Father, if it were possible, to take that cup (that painful experience) away. Then He made a statement that is the secret to managing our desires: "Nevertheless, not My will, but Yours, be done" (Luke 22:42). He dealt with His desires by submitting to the desires of the Father.

This is a statement we should keep in the handiest place in our minds: Not my will, Lord, but Yours, be done. God wants us to yield our will to His, and we don't need to forget it. We need to always be aware of it. Awareness, as a part of brilliant faith, requires remembering. We must remember what we know.

God instructed Joshua's generation of Israelites to meditate on God's Word day and night, to speak it day and night, and to write it on themselves. That was the most successful generation in Israel's history. Whatever it takes to remember God's most important words, we need to do. It will make the difference between life and death.

> When we say, "Not my will, Lord, but Yours, be done," it will always lead to life.

When we compare Jesus' garden example to Eve's garden example, it's clear that choosing God's will over our own faces us in the right direction. Eve's decision led to the original sin, bringing death to humankind. Jesus' decision led to obedience and brought life to humanity. Saying, "Not my will, Lord, but Yours, be done," will always lead to life.

Key #2 – Delight in the Lord

In Psalms 37 God gave us the secret to a "fulfilling desires" life. This is another truth we need to store into our Familiar bank and not forget to pull it up: "Delight yourself in the Lord and He will give you the desires of your heart" (Psalms 37:4).

This promise is ambiguous in an effective way. First, as we find our delight in God, He will establish in us new desires that match up with what He wants for us. The second meaning is that He will fulfill the desires He has established in us. What a great promise! God will transform our desires, replacing the old ones—the ones we don't want anyway—with new ones that are completely good. Those desires He will fulfill because He likes them, and He has the power to satisfy them.

My mom once gave me an interesting piece of marriage advice. She said, "The best way to get what you want is to want what your wife wants."

It's true. As I've grown to know Sharlene better and better and have come to love her even more through the years, my desires have come increasingly in line with hers (and hers with mine). Naturally, we help each other fulfill our common desires. This is like the principle of Psalm 37:4.

The desires God gives us are perfect, and He is fully capable of fulfilling all of them. Also, He is more likeable than any other. The better we get to know Him, the more desirable He is to us.

> **The desires God gives us are perfect, and He is fully capable of fulfilling all of them.**

Through the process of becoming more familiar with God, we find our "desires life" transformed into something beautiful.

When I think of delighting in the Lord, I think of King David dancing with all his might as he and the nation of Israel brought the ark of God's presence into the city of Jerusalem. He was so overjoyed to have God dwelling with him that he took off his royal clothing and danced with all the power he had.

Nothing else was so important to him as God's presence,

including his royalty and what anyone might think of him. That's when we know our delight is in the Lord, when His presence excites us more than anything else could. When we find ourselves there, our joy is full, and our desires are fulfilled.

Key #3 – Be Filled with the Spirit

While we aren't on the topic in this chapter of demon possession or casting out demons, the following Scripture contains a principle we can apply to our "desires life." Jesus said:

> *When an evil spirit leaves a person, it goes into the desert, searching for rest. But when it finds none, it says, 'I will return to the person I came from.' So it returns and finds that its former home is all swept and in order. Then the spirit finds seven other spirits more evil than itself, and they all enter the person and live there. And so that person is worse off than before* (Luke 11:24-26).

Jesus is addressing the danger of having a vacuum in our hearts. A vacuum is a space that contains no matter and no pressure. The danger of a vacuum in our psycho-spiritual life is that it can be filled with something destructive. When God helps us remove our ungodly desires, it's extremely important that we keep our hearts filled up with Him and that we don't allow destructive desires to reenter that space.

Paul simplified the solution for preventing a vacuum in our hearts in his letter to the Ephesians: "Be filled with the Spirit" (Eph. 5:18). In fact, the context of that statement is not to be filled with something destructive (in that case, not to be drunk with alcohol), but to fill that space with the Holy Spirit.

What we allow to occupy our hearts is critical. Romans 8:5-6 says,

> *For those who live according to the flesh set their minds on the things of the flesh, but those who live according to the Spirit, the*

things of the Spirit. For to be carnally minded is death, but to be spiritually minded is life and peace.

We all have conflicting desires at war within us, but we who have brilliant faith in Jesus have a decided advantage: we have the Holy Spirit residing in us. Paul wrote about that conflict and the importance of taking advantage of the indwelling Spirit:

I say then: Walk in the Spirit, and you shall not fulfill the lust of the flesh. For the flesh lusts against the Spirit, and the Spirit against the flesh; and these are contrary to one another, so that you do not do the things that you wish (Gal. 5:16-17).

For me, one of the most frustrating things is not to make good decisions because my ungodly desires are too strong. It's futile to do spiritual battle when my own desires are against me. A wise warrior establishes an advantage for himself before he engages in battle. He wants the victory to come as easily as possible, without having to depend on heroics. Heroic stories are great, but they are far outnumbered by stories of warriors losing against advantaged opponents.

As we walk in step with the Holy Spirit, He gives us the advantage in our combat against our ungodly desires. He weakens them and strengthens in us the desires He wants us to have. The way He does this is by leading us to feed our godly desires and starve our ungodly ones. The more we satisfy our Spirit-established desires, the stronger they are. The more we satisfy our flesh-established ones, the stronger they are. The Spirit of God gently guides us to feed the desires He wants us to have.

There's a great conflict taking place both within us and outside us. Outside, opponents vie to turn our desires in their direction. Within us rages the battle of conflicting desires. Let's stay ever conscious of these three thoughts:

1. Yielded: not my will, Lord, but Yours, be done!
2. Delighted: Lord, You are my greatest delight!
3. Filled: Holy Spirit, fill me and lead me!

Personal Application

- Journal about a desire you've struggled with that you know isn't a godly one. Include a request for God to replace that desire with one that He wants for you. Then continue—however long it takes—to write about the new desire and how things are different now.

–18–

Eyes

*Brilliant faith helps us see what God wants us to see,
the way He wants us to see it.*

There are two primary questions concerning our eyes: 1) *What* are we looking at? 2) *How* are we looking at it? The first question has to do with what's in front of our eyes. The second is concerned with what's behind them. The eye is the window to the soul, meaning our eyes have a profound impact on the contents of our hearts. With a fully functioning faith in Jesus, brilliant faith, our eyes will help us with far more than seeing.

I moved my family to Wilmington, North Carolina, in 2002 where we launched Grace Harbor Church. One day during our prelaunch preparation phase, my twelve-year-old son, Nathan, and I were crossing Market Street, one of the busiest streets in the city. It was at a point where the street was five lanes wide and with no pedestrian crossing lanes within more than a mile. Traffic was so thick that we had to cross one lane at a time, stopping to make sure the next lane was open before dashing across it. Once we got all the way across the street, Nate said to me, "I wasn't even watching the cars. I was just watching you and made sure I stayed close to you."

"Why did you watch me instead of the cars?" I asked.

"Because the Lord wants you to plant a church, and you haven't planted it yet."

I was impressed with Nate's faith, although not comfortable that it rested so much on me. But it was a fitting example for me, that I should keep my eyes so trustingly on the Lord when navigating through challenging situations.

Respect

I am blessed with a wife who loves me. One of the ways I know that is by what she does with her eyes. When she rises in the morning, I've usually been up for a while. Once I hear her enter the room, I look up and our eyes meet. She has looked for me, and she comes to me for a good morning kiss and hug.

Sometimes we meet at an event where lots of people are present, but when she enters the room, she looks for me and finds me. It doesn't matter how spectacular the event or what impressive person is there, she looks for me. Nobody else, nothing else. Me. Anytime we are across a room from each other, I can count on looking over and making eye contact with her. She usually won't go very long without looking my way.

This is no testament to my worthiness—I'm humbled by it. Rather, it speaks of her intentional love for and steadfast commitment to me, the one to whom she has given herself for life. She has decided in her heart to love me, and she has proven it in the smallest yet surest of ways: she always looks for me. You can tell what a person values, desires, and loves by watching their eyes.

> You can tell what a person values, desires, and loves by watching their eyes.

I love the picture painted by the word *respect*. The two parts of the word are *re*, meaning "again" and *spect*, meaning "look" or "see." To respect means we look to repeatedly.

We see it in basketball games when a player looks over at the coach to see what play to run, what advice he has, or what comfort he would give. Some players avoid looking to the sideline for fear of criticism or being taken out of the game. Some ignore their coach because they want to do things their own way, thinking the coach wouldn't support it. Players who have a good relationship with their coach look to them often and can institute their plans for the game. We often call that kind of player a coach on the floor or an extension of the coach.

Respect shows up clearly sometimes in little kids. A family is visiting in someone's home and the host offers the little five-year-old a piece of candy. The child immediately looks over at the parent to see if they're allowed to take a piece.

"You can have one. What do you say to Mrs. Williams?"

Respect is a beautiful thing.

Familiar and aware, we look to God. We invoke Him, trust Him, and heed Him. That's brilliant faith, and brilliant faith respects the Lord. It happens in our hearts, and it happens with our eyes because we respect Him in our hearts. He provides guidance for us. His guidance covers all areas of our lives, including our eyes. He lets us know where to land our eyes and how to interpret what we're seeing.

Spirit-Lens Perspective

A few years ago, my favorite work spot was the window table in the Port City Java on the corner of Grace and Front streets in Wilmington. Sitting at the table, I had an excellent view of the busy intersection, yet I was tucked in the corner of the coffee shop in a way that provided a quaint privacy, perfect for writing. One morning I sat there preparing my sermon for the upcoming Sunday. As I stopped and looked out the window to give my mind a break, I saw a man sitting on the other side of the window with his back to me. We were so close that were it not for the glass, I could have reached out and tapped him on the shoulder. He had positioned himself behind the cover of a small ornamental tree and was directing a hand-size video camera toward the opposite corner of the intersection. I looked at the LCD screen and saw that he was secretly videoing two people, a man and a woman, across the way.

I peered across the street and saw the two of them standing about ten feet apart, facing away from each other, the man to the north up Front Street and the woman to the east down Grace Street. She gave the appearance of being on her mid-morning work break, standing with her arms crossed, smoking a cigarette. His stance and his attire were casual. He looked up at the buildings and then down at the people on the street, up and down, back and forth, as if he were just out taking in the sights. But I could see that he was discreetly saying something each time he turned her way and that she spoke back. Both kept their comments short, never making eye contact, apparently suspicious of being watched.

In a few minutes, she finished her cigarette, dropped it, and stepped on it. Then each spoke a final word, turned, and looked ever so briefly into each other's eyes, a parting gesture neither could seem to resist. Finally, they turned and walked away from each other, him down Grace toward the river and into the parking deck and her down Front, getting back to work from her smoke break. The undercover camera guy, whom I had surmised to be a private investigator (I know, my instincts are impeccable), widened his lens and captured the man and the woman walking until they both disappeared from his screen.

Once they were out of sight, he flipped the LCD screen shut, bagged the camera, and disappeared.

I sat and processed what I had witnessed. Something hidden had been discovered, and I had the very distinct privilege of sharing in the perspective of the one who exposed it. Being in sermon prep mode, I did what most preachers do: I quickly produced a plan to use this fascinating experience as a sermon illustration. The parallel was immediately obvious. The private investigator represented the Holy Spirit. The cheating couple across the street, whom nobody knew about except for the PI and me, represented a reality, a truth that could be revealed only by God. The profound lesson was that the Holy Spirit would reveal hidden treasures of wisdom and knowledge to us if we would use our faith to position ourselves in His presence.

Recognizing the presence of the Holy Spirit and responding to Him appropriately (Invoke, Trust, and Heed) will position us to witness and experience the secret treasures that only He can offer. Those treasures are far more significant than seeing two unfaithful people sneak away to steal a moment on a street corner, although I'm sure that was significant to the spouses who were connected to them.

The treasures God will show us include a verse in the Bible we see in a way that we've never seen before that sheds timely light on an important part of our lives; a facial expression from a friend, letting us know they're hurting and need our help; a sky at dusk that somehow reminds us that He hasn't forgotten us and that He still paints tailor-made skies or provides whatever we really need.

Look Away

One of the many trade skills my dad developed was welding. As a young man he took a welding class and got a job as a welder to supplement his farming income. Years later, it came in handy as we built and repaired much of the equipment we used on the farm. Since I never mastered the craft, my job was usually to hold something in place while he welded it. He would always tell me, "Look away. Don't look at the arc now." I heard him say a dozen times, "I looked at the arc one time and that night it felt like I had sandspurs in my eyes."

That sandspurs comment never meant that much to me until one night after we had done some metal work. I had spent hours holding and hammering while my dad did the welding. Of course, I didn't look at the arc, I mean, what was I, stupid? I looked away just as I always had. But the arc reflected off the aluminum walls of the shop where we were working. I saw the reflection; it covered every inch of the walls, so it was everywhere. It was a mere reflection, so I didn't give it any thought. Sandspurs. That's exactly what it felt like, a hundred little prickly spur points dancing all over my eyeballs. I didn't sleep that night.

Gazing at images forbidden by God, like the millions of pornographic photos and videos available at the touch of a smartphone screen, bring prickly consequences. Imprinted indelibly onto the memory of our hearts, each one of those images tarnishes the vision we have of ourselves and others and presents formidable challenges to our relationship with God and our present, future, or possible spouses.

When Michael Jordan played in the NBA, some opposing coaches instructed their players to look away when Michael got free and went to the basket for a dunk. Those coaches didn't want their players to be awed by the elegance and power of one of his heroic, poetic flights punctuated with an electrifying slam. If opposing players saw too much of that from Jordan, they could become his captivated fans, rather than his fierce competitors.

Sometimes the best strategy for us against our enemy and his tactics is to look away. We can become awed at what we see, allowing ourselves to become captivated by our enemy. That level of awe we should reserve for God Himself. Where our eyes land can feed our hearts with life and faith, or lead us into bondage, destruction, and death. It can be challenging, but if we use it, brilliant faith will connect us with God and give us success in these battles.

Psalm 119:9 says "How can a young person stay pure? By obeying your word" (Ps. 119:9). Giving our eyes to the Word of God will prove to be protective and strengthening for us.

Proverbs 27:20 says, "Death and Destruction are never satisfied, and neither are the eyes of man."

Our eyes don't have to be used for death and destruction. Faith in Jesus connects us with Him and His power to overcome the relentless darkness of the world. If Christ lives in us and His Spirit is our predominant influence, the darkness will not be able to overtake us.

The light [Jesus Christ] *shines in the darkness, and the darkness can never extinguish it* (John 1:15 NLT).

The Power of Focus

I was a little frustrated when I learned that the driver's education class our oldest son, Sidney, was enrolled in included a mandatory class for the parents. *As if we aren't already busy enough,* I thought. Besides, I could teach the class, being the expert/professional-caliber driver that I was. Why did we have to go to this class? Well, that was one of my many times of prideful thinking, but God would soon humble me once again.

As the instructor went over some tips for supervising our kids' driving, he said something that I have never forgotten. Most people probably already know this, but somehow this rule had been lost on me. Addressing the need to pan your eyes back and forth across the lane you're driving in, he said, "Drivers tend to drive toward whatever they're looking at." My mind flashed back to the days of driving with my driver's permit. During a couple of the early weeks, as oncoming vehicles approached, I would veer closer to the yellow line and the approaching vehicle. Each time, understandably, my parents would panic.

"What are you doing? Stay away from the center line when cars are coming!"

It was so embarrassing. I was supposed to be a good driver before even taking driver's ed. I was raised on a farm, for crying out loud, and I had driven all kinds of vehicles off and on the road. There was no excuse for blunder, and I couldn't figure out why I was doing it. Eventually, I corrected it by just concentrating on staying far right of center, even if it meant running my right wheel off the road onto the shoulder. If I had understood the principle, "You tend to move in the direction of your focus," I would have been able to correct my problem very quickly. Now what I do is focus on the white line next to the shoulder while tracking the other car in my peripheral.

I've also taught that technique to my kids as they learned to drive, and I've used the principle (effectively, I think) in my teaching ministry over the years.

While that principle has applications in every area of our lives, it applies most directly to our eyes. If we focus our eyes sufficiently on God's Word, we will move effectively in the direction the Holy Spirit is leading us. If we place our focus on the images and messages of this world, we will move away from God and toward an eventual crash.

Our eyes will be drawn to things that match the contents of our hearts (TED). When I was in my twenties, I had a landscaping business. At that time in my life, everywhere I went, I noticed people's lawns and landscape design. As a pastor I notice church buildings. I never pay much attention to cars, but after I've just bought a car, I find myself noticing how many cars on the road are just like mine.

> **If we focus our eyes sufficiently on God's Word, we will move effectively in the direction the Holy Spirit is leading us.**

The same thing occurs with godly versus ungodly visuals that are filling up our hearts.

When our hearts are dominated by cravings for the impure and destructive, that's exactly where our eyes will land. Not only will they land on them, but if they aren't within our sight, we'll seek them out. That's why we can't forget the importance of filling our inner selves with the attributes of God.

Personal Application

- Take inventory of what your eyes take in daily and seek the Lord about whether you should make any adjustments.
- If you're willing, make a commitment that the first thing you'll set your eyes on each day is God's Word.

~19~

Ears

Our ears are the gateway for seeds of brilliant faith to enter.

It was not into my ear you whispered, but into my heart.
– Judy Garland

"We played the flute for you, and you did not dance; we sang a dirge, and you did not mourn" (Matt. 11:17 NIV).

Jesus stated the above words referring to the generation He dealt with during His earthly ministry years. They were complaining that He didn't listen to their dictates. It's true, He didn't seek their input. Rather, He sought His heavenly Father's. What Jesus listened to was the voice of the Father. God was the one He wanted to hear and please. The Gospels record that He stole away to be alone with the Father on more than one occasion, and I get the idea that ever present in His heart was the longing to fellowship privately with the Father.

Itchy

Because they have itching ears, they will heap up for themselves teachers; and they will turn their ears away from the truth and be turned aside to fables. But you be watchful in all things (2 Tim. 4:3-5).

Paul wrote prophetically to Timothy with a heads-up about how people would gather the messages they want to hear. Is it possible that there's never been a time when that was truer than it is today?

In an XM Radio interview, Billy Joel said there were times when other artists as well as himself didn't really care what their song lyrics said, if they sounded good. We make our own playlists and favorites and know where to tune in to hear the very words that will scratch our itchy ears, the voices that will say what we want to hear. To preface his warning, Paul instructed the young pastor Timothy to "Preach the word! Be ready in season and out of season" (2 Tim. 4:2).

Paul's instructions were to preach the always-true message of Jesus Christ, and to preach it whether it was popular to the fickle tastes of the culture or not. Our audio diet needs to be consistently godly and edifying. If we seek godly messaging only when we want to hear it, or when it happens to be celebrated, we'll find ourselves malnourished with no appetite for God. In contrast, a disciplined pursuit of God's Word in the music we listen to and the speakers and programming we choose to hear will help us stay healthy and hungry for God.

Familiar and aware are the two facets directly affected by ears. If what we hear builds our faith's basis and helps us to hear what God is saying to us in our current situation, our faith can be brilliant.

Personal Application

- What quality would you most like to have added to your character?

- Devise a strategy that includes what you'll listen to, as well as when and how often you'll listen to it, that will support adding that quality to yourself.

- Daily Prayer and Commitment: God, please speak to me what You want to say to me today. I commit to position myself to hear what You say.

- Daily Prayer and Commitment: God, above all other voices and sounds, I want to hear what You will say to me today. I will position myself, my ears and my heart, to hear what You will say. Thank You for the words You will send me!

—20—

Systems

Brilliant Faith sheds light on God's system for us.

Contrasting Kingdoms

The Bible presents two distinct kingdoms, each with its own king. God is king of the kingdom of heaven, and Satan's domain is the world. God both allows and establishes the limits of Satan's reign.

The World. The New Testament uses the word *world* in a couple of diverse ways. First, it uses it in a positive sense, as in John 3:16, declaring, "God so loved the world that He gave His only begotten Son, that whoever believes in Him will not perish, but have everlasting life." Here world refers to all the people in the world.

The second use has a negative meaning. For example, James 4:4-5 (NLT) warns: "If you want to be a friend of the world, you make yourself an enemy of God." It's the same word (world) as in John 3:16, and in both cases it's translated from the same Greek word. However, it obviously has different meanings in each of these verses, and the only way to know whether world is used in a positive sense or a negative sense is by its context.

I heard Pastor Tony Evans in one of his sermons define

world in its negative sense as "that system that leaves God out." I like that definition. When we read "world" in the New Testament, it comes from one of three Greek words, which combine to provide a complete understanding of the word:

The Earth. The Greek word *oikoumene* means "the whole inhabited earth," according to Strong's. So, where it's translated into the English world, it refers to all the people in the world.

The Age. The Greek word *aion*, from which we get our English word ion, means "age." It refers to the time when this globe and its inhabitants exist together.

The System. *Kosmos* is a Greek word that means "order, system, or arrangement." From it we get the word cosmos, and we use it in reference to the structure and order of the universe, it being so ingeniously designed and arranged.

Contrasting Mentalities

Those who live according to the flesh set their minds on the things of the flesh, but those who live according to the Spirit, the things of the Spirit (Rom. 8:5-6).

When a person puts their faith in Jesus Christ, the Spirit of God comes to dwell within them. Therefore, God is with and within us to do the ministry He desires to do in and for us. In the above verse, when God presents two choices of how to live and think, one of them—the one He obviously desires for us—is in cooperation with His Spirit. The other choice is in cooperation with the flesh. The meaning and use of the flesh is like the use of the world in its negative sense, in that it has a literal and a figurative meaning, the figurative being the more important one. The literal meaning of the flesh is "the parts, tissue, etc. of the human body." Remembering Tony Evans' definition of world, the figurative meaning is "that part of a person that wants to leave God out." You could say it's the world's spirit, as opposed to God's Spirit, in us. It's a mentality we construct by choosing to omit God in the decisions we make.

The Five Facets

Brilliant faith works by and gains strength from walking in step with the Spirit. Let's look at the benefits of walking in the Spirit in connection with the five facets of brilliant faith.

Familiar. The Holy Spirit has been given to us to "guide [us] into all truth" (John 16:13).

As we walk in step with Him, He guides us into increased understanding of truth about God. As that happens, our knowledge of God, the basis of our faith, expands.

Aware. As we walk in step with the Spirit, who lives inside us, we have a heightened awareness of His presence, His will, and His involvement in our situation.

Invoke. What a confidence we have in calling upon the Lord when we're in step with His very Spirit!

Trust. It's easier to trust God when we're closer to Him.

Heed. When we're in step with the Holy Spirit, hearing and heeding Him is a natural process.

Personal Application

- In what ways are you sometimes tempted to leave God out of your decision-making?
- According to Galatians 5:22, the fruit of the Spirit is love, joy, peace, patience, kindness, goodness, faithfulness, gen-

tleness, and self-control. Take a personal inventory and prayerfully judge the production of the Spirit's fruit in your life. Ask God to help you in the areas that are deficient. As you walk in step with the Spirit going forward, be prepared for His guidance in the areas you've asked.

~21~

Tongue

When brilliant faith wields the tongue,
the results are life and power.

Jesus said that people's words flow from the contents of their hearts (Luke 6:45). If our hearts are full of brilliant faith, our words flow from being familiar with God, being aware of Him, and our trust in Him. With our words, we invoke and we heed Him. Heeding words declare His power, love, desires, and benefits. A heart without faith, on the other hand, produces words that lack His power, love, desires, and benefits. A heart full of faith is key to speaking the most positive, constructive words possible.

Proverbs 18:21 says, "Life and death are in the power of the tongue." Our words are powerful, whether flowing from a heart filled with faith or from a heart filled with doubt, fear, anxiety, or confusion. The choice is ours. The Lord instructs us to "choose life" (Deut. 30:19). The most constructive words are those spoken from a heart filled with faith.

Brilliant faith equips us to speak the most productive words because by faith we're able to speak God's words. When we speak God's words, it's as if He's speaking them with our mouths; He makes us His mouthpiece. We get to participate in the most powerful process in existence: the process of God sending His Word. Look what happens when God sends His Word:

> *Just as rain and snow descend from the skies and don't go back until they've watered the earth, doing their work of making things grow and blossom, producing seed for farmers and food for the hungry, so will the words that come out of my mouth not come back empty-handed. They'll do the work I sent them to do, they'll complete the assignment I gave them* (Isa. 55:10-11 MSG).

Five Categories of Listeners in Your Audience

Think of yourself as being a speaker. In your audience there are five distinct categories of listeners: God and heaven, other people, yourself, Satan and hell, and Things. Your words have the power to affect everyone in your audience in every category.

1. God and heaven

Jesus made a promise to His disciples. "Whatever you ask in My name I will do" (John 14:14 Phillips). Once He went to the Father and sent the Holy Spirit, which is our current era, His promise would take effect. The words of request we speak in the name of Jesus are always honored. What power those words have!

Jesus also promised us that heaven's immense power will conduct the righteous decrees we make. "Whatever you bind on earth will be bound in heaven and whatever you loose on earth will be loosed in heaven" (Matt. 16:19). Of course, His promise isn't for rogue decision-making and words with ungodly motives. The promise applies to us when we are in step with the Holy Spirit, having the mind of Christ and acting within the purview of His will.

An angel came to Daniel to give him the understanding he was seeking from God. "From the first day that you set your heart to understand, and to humble yourself before your God, your words were heard; and I have come because of your words" (Dan. 10:12). Who knows what celestial forces God mobilizes, what angelic rulers He dispatches, what critical missions He assigns in response to our words of faith? My faith tells me that it's significant!

One of the most prominent communications God wants to hear from us is confession when we've sinned. While God instructs us in His Word to confess our sins to each other, the most important ears to hear us confess are His. Sometimes acknowledging wrong is hard to do, but once we get the words out, a freedom and a cleanliness follow that can't be found elsewhere.

Our family vehicle for several years was a fifteen-passenger van. One evening our family had eaten out with friends. After dinner, as we were all getting into the van, Sharlene and I discovered that someone had punctured a hole in one of the van seats. It was the seat where our youngest, Janna, five years old at the time, normally sat. We asked Janna if she had done it, and she said she hadn't. We all climbed into the van, and I drove us home. On the twenty-minute trip home, I tried to find the underlying cause of what caused the hole. All five of Janna's siblings said they saw her earlier that day cutting some paper with a pair of scissors in the very seat that was punctured. The small hole looked exactly like it had been done with scissors. Janna still denied doing it. As I questioned all the other kids, Kristin, who always shared a seat with Janna, told me she looked over and saw Janna pulling the scissors out of the seat earlier that day.

"I didn't do it," Janna maintained.

It was clear to me, though, as well as everyone else in the family, that she had done it.

"Janna, we all know you did it. Just go ahead and admit it," Sharlene said.

"I didn't do it."

I really wanted Janna to tell the truth, so I decided to make it easy for her, "Janna, we all know you did it, and you know it too. If you'll confess that you did it, there won't be any consequences. If you don't tell the truth, you'll have to get a spanking when we get home."

"I didn't do it."

All Janna's siblings began working frantically to convince her to confess, "Just tell Dad you did it, and you won't get a spanking."

"I didn't do it."

All the other kids were in a panic. "Just tell him, Janna. Just tell him! If you don't, you'll get a spanking!"

"I didn't do it."

We turned off the main road and into our subdivision. I said, "Janna, I want to make sure you understand this. We all know you put the hole in the seat. It was probably an accident, and that's okay. But you need to tell the truth before we get home, or you'll get a spanking because you've got to learn to tell the truth, even when it's hard."

"I didn't do it."

Noise levels in the van went dangerously high, as the five older kids yelled and pleaded to convince Janna to confess what she'd done.

"I didn't do it."

"Janna, we're about to turn onto our street," I said. "You

need to tell the truth before we get home."

"I didn't do it."

We turned onto our street. The second house on the left was ours. Time was about to run out.

We all felt sorry for Janna and tried desperately to convince her. We were a few feet from our driveway, and all the shouting died down.

I delivered one final pitch. "Janna, you need to tell me the truth before we turn into the driveway so you won't get a spanking."

Janna spoke in the softest, most sheepish little voice, "I did it."

Everyone was so relieved. We all celebrated and congratulated Janna on telling the truth and avoiding a spanking.

As hard as it is sometimes to confess our sins, it's much easier when we know we won't be condemned. Janna felt the same freedom I've felt many times after speaking the truth to God about my sins. He's the most important and most supportive member in our audience.

2. Other people

The Bible makes our relationship with God the number-one priority for us, but second and inseparably connected to the first, is our treatment of each other. You could say that the overarching theme of the Bible is: First, love God. Second, love people. Love doesn't just lie dormant in our hearts. Like faith, it manifests.

One of the primary ways we show love to people is with our words. When we speak to someone, we're imparting something to them. We're sending something from our minds to theirs, but what impact will it have on them? Will it build them up, like super-nutrients for their hearts? Or will it tear them down, like a debilitating virus? We can spread life or disease in people's hearts.

We have the power to add courage to people. We can open their eyes to what God can do in their life. We can help them gain confidence in who they are and what they can do. We can affirm them by reminding them of their strengths and accomplishments. We can remind them that people in their life love them. We can help them remember that God values them, is for them, and is still working for their good. We can do all this with our words.

As I was writing this very paragraph just now, my wife brought her phone over to me and said,

"You need to watch this." (She had no idea what I was writing.)

I took her phone and touched play on the screen. A little boy, five or six years old, was in a martial arts class. He was trying to break a board with his foot. He tried several times, but his kicks were too weak and he couldn't do it. His instructor, who was holding the board, said, "You can do it, but kick it with your heel, and you have to kick it hard."

He tried several more times, one time losing his balance and falling, but his kicks weren't any stronger, and he couldn't break the board.

Embarrassed, he began to cry. His instructor wasn't letting him off the hook, though. He knew the boy could do it, and he kept reminding him so.

His classmates began chanting his name. His instructor shouted louder; he had to, because the other students were chanting the boy's name louder and louder. The instructor shouted, "You can do it! Kick it hard with your heel!"

He kicked it harder. And then harder. You could see his courage and determination growing as everyone cheered him on. Finally, he delivered the decisive blow, and the board split in two.

His classmates swarmed him, hugged him, and patted him on the back. His face said it all. He went from tears to laughter, from discouragement to victory, in less than a minute—all because of the simple encouraging words of the people who wanted him to succeed.

(Thanks, Sharlene, for the timely illustration. God is good!)

3. Yourself

When we speak to someone else, there's another person we don't usually think of who is also listening: we are. Everything we say goes into our own ears, and our words are just as powerful from our own mouths as from someone else's. We should consider ourselves as another category in our audience.

With that in mind, I recommend that we talk to ourselves. I know a lot of people do that, but I think it's usually just processing our thoughts by speaking them—thinking aloud, as the expression goes. We should be more intentional about it. We should speak not just to speak out our thoughts, but to hear the words we need to hear.

David modeled this in Psalms 42, 103, and 104. In Psalm 42:5-6 he wrote: "Why are you downcast, O my soul? Why so disturbed within me? Put your hope in God, for I will yet praise him, for the help of His countenance."

David wrote Psalm 103 to himself. He instructed himself to bless the Lord and not to forget all the Lord's benefits. Then he set out to name the benefits that we have in the Lord. He began his instructions to himself with these words:

Bless the Lord, O my soul; and all that is within me, bless His holy name! Bless the Lord, O my soul, and forget not all His benefits (Ps. 103:1-2).

Talking to ourselves isn't only for people with mental issues. It's also for people with all other kinds of issues, the kind we all have, the kind that keep us from walking with God in faith. We can't always wait for someone else to speak what we need to hear. Sometimes we need to tell ourselves what we need to hear.

4. Satan and hell

We have two examples in the Bible of people in conversation with Satan. One was a "how to" and the other was a "how not to." The "how not to" was Eve in Eden with the serpent (Gen. 3). Her mistake was accepting the serpent's words instead of continuing to speak God's words to him. The result was a huge failure. The "how to" was Jesus in the wilderness (Luke 4). His success was in His speaking of God's Word, rather than accepting the words of the devil.

> **It would be tragic to have such a powerful weapon as God's Word, only to have our enemy dominate us because we won't use it.**

Jesus commanded him to leave. Jesus has given us His name and His authority to overcome our enemy. Speaking words of faith from a heart that serves the King of Kings is one of the ways we overcome him. We need to remind our enemy that the one who lives in us, the Spirit of Christ, is greater than he is (1 John 4:4). We may need to reinform him that any weapon formed against us will not succeed (Isaiah 54:17). The enemy can be quieted by the sword of the

Spirit, which is the Word of God. It would be tragic to have such a powerful weapon as God's Word, only to have our enemy dominate us because we won't use it.

My dad once said to a man, "Do you know how I can tell you're lying? Because your lips are moving."

We must remember that when we encounter something contrary to God's Word, it's from Satan and it's a lie. Our recourse is to speak God's Word to him, to quiet him, so he can't cause us confusion. We must make him a hearer in our audience and not let him have the microphone.

5. Things

We've addressed all the persons in our audience, but one category remains. If you had trouble with the idea of speaking to yourself or to Satan, this one may be a real stretch for you. I'm talking about speaking to things. Before you reject the idea, let me support it soundly with Scripture.

Jesus spoke to a storm, commanding it to be still, and it obeyed Him. He informed His disciples that with faith they could speak to mountains and trees, commanding them to move, and they would obey them. Was Jesus using hyperbole to help us understand that we can do remarkable things with our faith? Was He using the mountain and the tree as mere symbols of more realistic, figurative mountains and trees, like massive challenges, tricky situations? My answer to both those questions is no.

Then He arose and rebuked the wind, and said to the sea, "Peace, be still!" And the wind ceased and there was a great calm (Mark 4:39).

If you have faith as a mustard seed, you will say to this mountain, "Move from here to there," and it will move; and nothing will be impossible for you (Matt. 17:20).

If you have faith and do not doubt, you will not only do what was done to the fig tree, but also if you say to this mountain, 'Be removed and be cast into the sea,' it will be done (Matt. 21:21).

If you have faith as a mustard seed, you can say to this mulberry tree, "Be pulled up by the roots and be planted in the sea," and it will obey you (Luke 17:6).

I've spoken to storms, and they've obeyed me. I didn't speak to them as an experiment or for my own entertainment but for the purpose of letting people know at outdoor events we had planned that Jesus loves them. I've been a part of trusting God to remove some mountainous obstacles, like a tumor from my daughter-in-law, Haley's, brainstem, and a lack of financial resources. We tried to let our words be words of faith in those situations, but I've never needed to move a literal mountain or have a tree transplanted from the land into the sea. If I ever do, I hope I'll use my faith words to do it.

We need to speak to the mountains, the trees, the storms, the obstacles that stand in the way of God's victory in our lives. I'm in a season now of faith-speaking. Some situations in my life are mountainous, and I want them removed. They have to do with the eternal salvation of some people I love very much, some marriages that are being ravaged by our enemy, and some opportunities to help people grow in their relationship with Jesus. I won't name those people here, but I invite you to add your faith to mine for these situations. Please and thank you!

Personal Application

- Take time every day to speak to all five types of listeners in your audience. Be sure your speeches are faith-filled and based on the Word of God.

—22—

Extremities

Brilliant faith can influence where we go and what we do.

*Extremities represent our hands and feet—
where we go and what we do.*

Where We Go

Brilliant faith will have profound influence on our decisions about where we go.

Abram and his nephew, Lot, had both outgrown the land they shared. Their herds and flocks were too big, and their shepherds and herders were in conflict. So, Abram invited Lot to choose his preferred land and expand onto it. Then Abram would take what was left.

> *And Lot lifted his eyes and saw all the plain of Jordan, that it was well watered everywhere (before the Lord destroyed Sodom and Gomorrah) like the garden of the Lord, like the land of Egypt as you go toward Zoar. Then Lot chose for himself all the plain of Jordan, and Lot journeyed east. And they separated from each other. Abram dwelt in the land of Canaan, and Lot dwelt in the cities of the plain and pitched his tent even as far as Sodom. But the men of Sodom were exceedingly wicked and sinful against the Lord* (Gen. 13:10-13).

Lot didn't rely on what he knew about God (familiar). Nor did he consider that God was present and available to lead him in his decision (aware). Lot didn't consult God regarding his choice (invoke). Since he was neither familiar, aware, nor interactive with the Lord, he didn't trust Him or heed Him. Operating without brilliant faith, Lot chose foolishly, which led to much trouble in his life. He ended up narrowly escaping the destruction of Sodom, fleeing for his life, and losing his wife.

Therefore hear me now, my children, and do not depart from the words of my mouth. Remove your way far from her, and do not go near the door of her house (Prov. 5:7-8).

King Solomon designated the entire fifth chapter of Proverbs to warning readers about the perils of getting involved with an adulterous woman. I think it's significant that he stated in the above excerpt the danger of going not into her bed but near the door of her house. Being familiar with this warning from God, listening for His voice in decisions about situations where danger could lurk, calling to Him for help, trusting His instructions, and responding obediently to Him means that brilliant faith is at work for our safety and guidance.

In this case, as with the case of Lot, the lesson is to steer clear of ungodliness, to keep ourselves several steps away from the actual danger, not to find ourselves even in the vicinity of it. Even when we can't foresee trouble down a given path, we can trust the one who can. Nothing is hidden from God; fortunately, He's more than willing to warn us by His Word and by His Spirit. The key is to walk in brilliant faith, remembering what we've learned from God, being aware of and alert to His presence and leading, calling upon Him for insight, trusting Him, and heeding Him. That's infinitely more effective than leaning on our insufficient knowledge and understanding.

Entreat me not to leave you, or to turn back from following after you; for wherever you go, I will go; and wherever you lodge, I

will lodge; your people shall be my people, and your God, my God
(Ruth 1:16).

The story of Ruth is about a young widow repeatedly po-
sitioning herself where she could receive and enjoy the blessings of God. Ruth stubbornly attached herself to her Jewish
mother-in-law, Naomi, leaving her own people to become a
part of God's chosen people. Then she positioned herself in
the graces of the wealthy and respectable Boaz, who made her
his wife, and followed the advice of the godly Naomi and Jesus
of Nazareth, the Savior of the world.

Speaking of Jesus, He established for us the basic principle
of where to go to be intricately connected with God. He was
in dialogue with a Samaritan woman at a well just outside the
city of Sychar. Being a Samaritan, the woman asserted that
God should be worshiped in Samaria, rather than in Jerusalem
where the Temple stood.

Jesus clarified for her that Jerusalem was, for that time, the
place of worship. Then He spoke of a time soon to come, the
age we now live in now, when worshiping God wouldn't be
limited to any location but at any place where people sought
His omnipresent Spirit.

> *Woman, believe Me, the hour is coming when you will neither
> on this mountain, nor in Jerusalem, worship the Father. You
> worship what you do not know; we know what we worship, for
> salvation is of the Jews. But the hour is coming, and now is,
> when the true worshipers will worship the Father in spirit and
> truth; for the Father is seeking such to worship Him. God is
> Spirit, and those who worship Him must worship in spirit and
> truth* (John 4:21-24).

Since God will lead us to, or away from, certain places by
His Spirit, where we really want to be positioned is by His

Spirit. Where we go isn't geographical as much as it is spiritual. God wants us to worship Him in Spirit. What we need to do is to seek His presence; we can seek, find, and worship Him without geographical limitation.

What We Do

Whatever you do, do all to the glory of God (1 Cor. 10:31-32).

As Paul wrote in his first letter to the Corinthian church, the secret to doing what is right is to do everything for God's glory. If we run every action through the filter of its giving God credit and honor, we'll find our lives filled up with right and God-honoring actions. If our faith is brilliant, God can give us the insight we need to glorify Him with what we do.

Personal Application

- At the end of each day, pinpoint on a map the places you went that day. Answer why you went there. Note whether each was for a godly purpose. Learn from the mistakes or patterns you see and consider what you've learned to improve decisions about where you go.

- Invoke God to direct you to actions that will bring Him honor and notoriety and to direct you away from any action that would undermine His glory. Be sensitive to His response and ready to heed His direction.

-23-

Resources

*Everything in our lives is a resource we can use
for God with brilliant faith.*

Resources consist of everything we can access, influence, or control to any degree and in any way. Everything about us, tangible or intangible, every faculty of our inner life (TED) is a resource. Every part of our personality is a resource, and every member of our physical bodies is a resource. Whatever we take in, everything we admit into our minds or our bodies, each one is a resource. Everything we can see, hear, or sense in any way, each becomes a resource for us. Every person and every relationship with each person, regardless of the nature of that relationship, is a resource. Every responsibility, privilege, experience, talent, freedom, pain, victory, influence, every second of time—all are resources.

Our homes, vehicles, jobs, businesses, assets, credit, devices, pets, and neighborhoods are all resources. Every place where we can go, whether we own it or are allowed there as guests, citizens, or patrons—places like parks, restaurants, highways, retail and services locations, websites, beaches, arenas, fairgrounds, hiking trails—all are resources. Everything we use, whether we purchase it, borrow it, or make it is a resource.

Virtually everything in our lives is a resource. The sheer number of resources in our lives is more than we can comprehend. Equally mindboggling are all the possibilities our resources afford us. We have millions of options available to us. The biggest question is how we'll manage them.

Paul established faith, hope, and love as supremely important (1 Cor. 13:13). I think we could say that outside of God Himself and the eternal relationship we have with Him as Christians, those three are our greatest resources. They are an integral part of our relationship with Him. The reason they are so important is because they determine more than anything else how we deal with our resources.

Brilliant faith has a profound impact on our resources in two ways: access and management. Many resources we can access only by faith, and they are the most valuable ones. Brilliant faith also transforms the way we manage our resources. Our entire approach to resources is completely different when we have brilliant faith.

Stewards Not Owners

Ownership is a status that gives us the highest level of freedom and control over possessions, but we never have absolute freedom and control. It's always possible to lose a resource, except the eternal gifts that God gives to us.

A nation state may claim sovereignty over its resources, thereby claiming ownership status. When another enemy state overpowers it and assumes control of its resources, it loses its sovereignty and the freedom and control it had in ownership status. Now its status has changed.

Sovereignty, along with all authority, belongs to God because He owns everything. God is the creator, the originator, of all resources. Any authority anyone has originated with Him, and He delegates it.

A hospital nurse has the authority to treat a patient because that patient consented to have the hospital care for them. The hospital delegates to the nurse the authority to treat the patient within the scope of his/her nursing license. The hospital received its authority from the government agency that regulates the nation's healthcare. That agency is empowered by the nation's governmental leaders. Those leaders and that nation were allowed by God the power and authority to exist and to govern.

> Sovereignty, along with all authority, ultimately belongs to God because He owns everything.

Every citizen of a nation accesses their resources according to the laws of the nation. God established the nation. He also works intricately in the citizens' lives to provide each with their resources. Everything we have comes from God, and He packs purpose into every resource. All our resources come from God, belong to God, and are purposed for God.

Therefore, every resource in our lives is something we have stewardship privileges and responsibilities over, regardless of whether we own it or someone else owns it. God owns each one, and we are accountable to Him for our management of it. By brilliant faith we understand our stewardship because of what we know about God, our trust in Him, and our life of responding to Him. By brilliant faith we are stewards, not owners. With our stewardship comes five necessary qualities:

1. Awareness of God's Ownership

When stewards see themselves as owners, they mismanage, misappropriate, and embezzle the owners' resources. In brilliant faith we know that God is the creator and owner of all things. We trust Him to provide for us, so we can be successful in our role of steward. We know that we don't own anything, even if we hold a title or deed to a property. Our children are His, our spouses and our friends are His, and He allows us to steward a special relationship with each. Even we are not our own—not our bodies, souls, or any part of us. We are His.

> *And what do you have that you did not receive? Now if you did indeed receive it, why do you boast as if you had not received it?* (1 Cor. 4:7)

2. Sense of Purpose

The owner gets to decide the purpose of His resources. By brilliant faith we know God purposes all things for His glory. That includes us; our purpose is to glorify Him. Since God created us for that purpose, we are most fulfilled by glorifying Him through living out our purpose. We're all different, each person a unique mixture of personality traits. Some of our personality traits are easier to manage than others. My youngest son, Luke, is talented and creative in several areas. He's won talent awards in singing, acting, writing, drawing, and photography. Yet he doesn't bask in the spotlight. He prefers to be out of the limelight. I tell him he has center stage talent with a backstage ego.

His personality makes it easier for him manage his talents. Talent is a resource exceedingly difficult for many people to submit to God.

> *For by Him all things were created that are in heaven and that are on earth, visible and invisible, whether thrones or dominions or principalities or powers. All things were created through Him and for Him* (Col. 1:16).

3. Sense of Responsibility

An ownership mentality leads us to think we don't have to report to anybody. We do what we want with our stuff. Conversely, by brilliant faith, we know that our stuff is really God's stuff, and we see the stuff from a unique perspective. Stewardship status is a humbler status than an ownership status, and humility helps us place ourselves rightly under God's authority. Recognizing His authority makes it natural for us to have a sense of responsibility to Him.

So then each of us shall give account of himself to God (Rom. 14:12-14 NLT).

4. Gratitude

When we understand that we didn't accomplish anything without God's help, it's only natural to have an intense sense of gratitude. The more aware we are of what God has done for us, the more thankful we're going to be.

Gratitude is valuable to us because it staves off any sense of entitlement, which is a debilitating mentality. Thankfulness is also valuable to God. Look at the fascinating idea Paul gave in his first letter to the church in Corinth. From this verse I picture a factory mass-producing thanksgivings. People are doing things for others and that produces gratefulness to God in the recipients of those acts. I see God being so pleased as He gathers up our expressions of gratitude. How awesome it is to give God joy!

Carrying out this social relief work involves far more than helping meet the bare needs of poor Christians. It also produces abundant and bountiful thanksgivings to God (2 Cor. 9:12 MSG).

5. Generosity

Sowing results in reaping. But the harvest for certain generosities is not for the sower. When we heed the Lord by faith, He will sometimes call us to such a generosity.

As a pastor, I once had a difficult person join my church leadership team. Although he had some great qualities, his greatest being his heart for God, he was stubborn and hard to work with at times. I sometimes complained to my wife how difficult he was at times as a team member.

One day the Lord directed my attention to this team member and said, "I brought you gold, and you've complained that you have to polish it."

Obviously, that changed my perspective about that person, as well as my expectation of him. However, I never saw a change in him and, consequently, he never met my revised expectations.

One day I asked, "Lord, how was [that person] gold to me?"

"He wasn't gold to you. He's gold to Me."

The Lord had called me to invest in one of his children. Yet I assumed that my investment would pay dividends to me. How arrogant and off the mark! What an unworthy steward I had been!

That person eventually moved on to launch an extremely valuable ministry. Had I understood he would do that, I would've invested more generously in him. Good stewards require only enough understanding to be obedient. As a good steward, I should've generously invested in my team member and left the return on investment up to the Lord. Look at what Jesus said:

> When you put on a luncheon or a banquet," he said, "don't invite your friends, brothers, relatives, and rich neighbors. For they will invite you back, and that will be your only reward. Instead, invite the poor, the crippled, the lame, and the blind. Then at the resurrection of the righteous, God will reward you for inviting those who could not repay you (Luke 14:13).

I also love God's logic when it comes to giving to the poor. He takes responsibility for repayment. Even though Jesus rescues us from the penalty for all our wrongs, He'll still see to it that we receive reward for our generosity.

If you help the poor, you are lending to the Lord—and He will repay you! (Prov. 19:17 NLT)

Son-Stewards

When we enter God's kingdom, we enter as sons. Why not sons and daughters? Why just sons?

Because in the culture of Bible times, sons were their parents' heirs. They were the recipients of the parents' estates. A daughter became part of her husband's family and didn't inherit anything from her parents.

Most modern translations of the Bible translate "sons and daughters" or "children" from the original sons to make it clear to our culture that male and female are equal heirs in Christ (Gal. 3:26-28). Here's how an older translation, NKJV, compares to a more modern one, NLT, in the way they translate Galatians 3:26-28:

NKJV	NLT
For you are all sons of God through faith in Christ Jesus. For as many of you as were baptized into Christ have put on Christ. There is neither Jew nor Greek, there is neither slave nor free, there is neither male nor female; for you are all one in Christ Jesus.	*For you are all children of God through faith in Christ Jesus. And all who have been united with Christ in baptism have put on the character of Christ, like putting on new clothes. There is no longer Jew or Gentile, slave or free, male and female. For you are all one in Christ Jesus.*

I'm glad translators use terminology to include male and female as equal heirs, so there's no confusion about that. What may not come through as loudly in those translations is this: God has given everyone the highest possible status through our faith in Jesus.

We are stewards but not mere stewards. We're son-stewards. If we see ourselves as mere stewards, we miss the fullness of the status God has reserved for us. Jesus made this point clear when He told the story of the prodigal son:

> *Then He said: "A certain man had two sons. And the younger of them said to his father, "Father, give me the portion of goods that falls to me." So he divided to them his livelihood. And not many days after, the younger son gathered all together, journeyed to a far country, and there wasted his possessions with prodigal living. But when he had spent all, there arose a severe famine in that land, and he began to be in want. Then he went and joined himself to a citizen of that country, and he sent him into his fields to feed swine. And he would gladly have filled his stomach with the pods that the swine ate, and no one gave him anything.*
>
> *"But when he came to himself, he said, 'How many of my father's hired servants have bread enough and to spare, and I perish with hunger! I will arise and go to my father, and will say to him, "Father, I have sinned against heaven and before you, and I am no longer worthy to be called your son. Make me like one of your hired servants." And he arose and came to his father. But when he was still a great way off, his father saw him and had compassion, and ran and fell on his neck and kissed him. And the son said to him, 'Father, I have sinned against heaven and in your sight, and am no longer worthy to be called your son.' But the father said to his servants, 'Bring out the best robe and put it on him, and put a ring on his hand and sandals on his feet. And bring the fatted calf here and kill it, and let us eat and be*

merry; for this my son was dead and is alive again; he was lost and is found.' And they began to be merry" (Luke 13:11-32).

The son didn't lose his son status, even though he felt he no longer deserved to have it. It's the same for us: when we come back to our Father by faith, He joyfully embraces us and restores our original status, the status we would've had if nobody had ever sinned. He does this because Jesus has regained that status for us by paying off our sin-debt on His cross.

As stewards of the resources in our lives, our son-status gives us interest beyond what we would have as mere stewards. I spent my teenage and early-twenties years working on our family farm. My dad also hired men to collaborate with us. Many of those men were conscientious and took immense pride in their work and in taking care of my dad's interests. However, Daddy always treated me differently. His expectation of me was that I approach everything exactly as he would. I may have worked alongside the men he hired, but I was his son. I had a much closer relationship with him; therefore, I had a different relationship to our resources. Our status as sons places in our hearts a love for our Father's interests and a different relationship to His resources. We aren't mere stewards; we're son-stewards. Whether male or female, we have the highest possible status through our faith. We have more than duty; we have heritage.

Personal Application

- Make a list of all the resources you can think of in your life. It'll help to set them up in categories such as tangible, intangible, relational, etc. Give some thought and prayer about how to best manage them.

Shine Forth

Go thou and be brilliant!

You are the light of the world. A city that is set on a hill cannot be hidden. Nor do they light a lamp and put it under a basket, but on a lampstand, and it gives light to all who are in the house. Let your light so shine before men, that they may see your good works and glorify your Father in heaven (Matt 5:14-16).

When Jesus spoke the above words, I believe He meant it for those who would believe in Him, those who would have genuine, complete faith in Him—brilliant faith. As we walk out our brilliant faith, its brilliance, the radiant light of Christ, will shine for people to see and glorify God by choosing Christ for themselves. Please be one of those people who heed what Jesus said. Happy shining!

About the Author

Gabriel and his wife of thirty-five years, Sharlene, live in Wilmington, NC. They have six grown children, three daughters-in-law, and four grandchildren (to whom they are known as G-Pop and Lolli).

Gabriel has been a musician, church planter, pastor, and healthcare administrator. He currently serves as Executive Director of Christian Recovery Houses, a discipleship ministry for people recovering from addiction.

Contact Information

Contact Gabriel at gabrieltew@gabrieltew.com
Or visit his website to read his blog and
order resources directly from him
at gabrieltew.com.